RICHMOND
PAST

A View from Richmond Hill, by Sir Joshua Reynolds – his only major landscape, painted from near his house. (Aquatint by William Birch, 1788.)

RICHMOND PAST

A Visual History
of Richmond
Kew, Petersham and Ham

by
John Cloake

HISTORICAL PUBLICATIONS

TO ELEANOR

First published 1991
by Historical Publications Ltd
32 Ellington Street, London N7 8PL
(Tel: 020 7607 1628)
Reprinted 1993, 1998, 2004

ISBN 0 948667 14 1

Typeset in Palatino by Historical Publications Ltd
Printed by South China Printing Company, Hong Kong/China

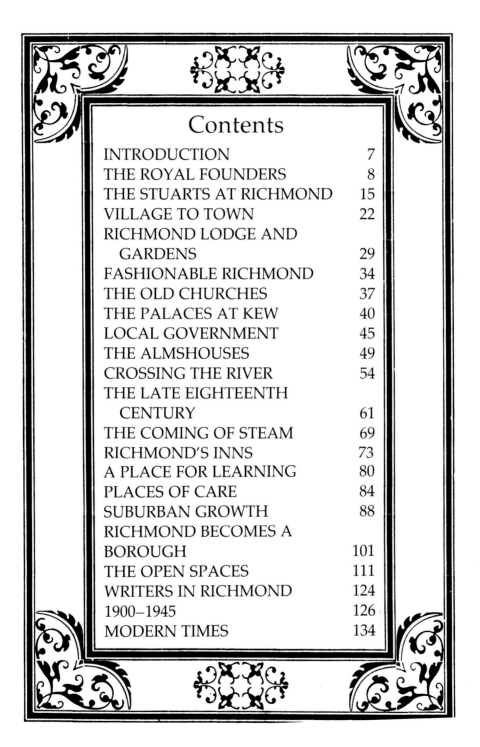

Contents

The Illustrations

The author and publisher are particularly indebted to the following for their co-operation in the assembly of the illustrations: Diana Howard, Principal Librarian, Reference and Information Services, and Jane Baxter, Local Studies Librarian, of the London Borough of Richmond upon Thames; Ruth de Iongh of the Orleans House Gallery; the Museum of Richmond; Bamber Gascoigne.

The following have kindly given their permission to reproduce illustrations:

The London Borough of Richmond upon Thames: jacket, 22, 24, 27, 29, 30, 32, 36, 38, 39, 48, 58, 59, 78, 79, 80, 83, 84, 93, 95, 97, 99, 106, 107, 117, 118, 121, 124, 126, 128, 129, 133, 135, 137, 140, 146, 148, 152, 161, 162, 163, 165, 172, 176, 181, 182, 184, 185, 187, 192, 195, 197, 198, 199, 203, 204, 205, 206, 208, 211, 219, 220, 237, 238, 239, 242, 243, 244, 246, 247, 248, 249, 253, 254, 255, 256, 266
The Museum of Richmond: 3, 6, 200
Bamber Gascoigne from his book *Images of Richmond* (1978): 8, 23, 28, 33, 45, 55, 85, 92, 96, 101, 104, 109, 116, 127, 134, 136, 138, 139, 147, 191, 207, 213, 218, 231, 233, 234, 241
The British Library, 1, 175
The British Museum, Prints and Drawings, 89, 94
The Ashmolean Museum, Oxford, 5
The Duke of Northumberland, 11 (with details shown at 52, 53, 73 and 75), 42
The National Portrait Gallery, 14, 110, 240
Victoria and Albert Museum, 17, 18
Lamport Hall Trustees, 20
Private Collections, 88, 103
Royal Institute of British Architects, 90
Stadilijke Museum, Amsterdam, 174
Richmond and Twickenham Times, 267
James Barron, 230
The Manager of Richmond Odeon, 245
Hampton's estate agents, 25
Richmond and Twickenham Photographic Society, 252
Phillimore & Co, 19

All other illustrations were supplied by the author or the publisher.

Introduction

Richmond, Surrey, did not exist as a place name until 1501, yet its recorded history goes back to the middle of the tenth century. It is one of the few English towns to have changed its name since the Middle Ages; and it did so at the whim of a King – Henry VII.

Richmond was known to the Anglo-Saxons and Normans as Shene, a name whose origins seem more likely to lie in the Anglo-Saxon word *sceo* meaning 'shelter' than in *sciene* meaning 'shining'. About AD950 Bishop Theodred of London made his will, in which among other properties he disposed of his holdings at Fulham, Wunemanedune (Wimbledon) and Sceon (Shene).

It may be that the manor house of the Anglo-Saxon kings' town (Kingston) was at Shene, for at the time of the Domesday Survey Shene was a part of that royal manor, as were Kew and Ham. Only Petersham had a separate manorial identity; it had been granted in the eighth century to Chertsey Abbey.

The names of Petersham (Patrice's homestead), Ham (a meadowland in a river bend) and Kew (anciently Cay-hoe – a projecting spur of land like a key or peg) are equally of Saxon origin. A 'visual history' can however present little of the period before the sixteenth century, for Richmond has no medieval ruins standing above the surface of the ground.

Nevertheless our story must start with the medieval royal palaces of Shene, for they were the focus and *raison d'être* of the village that became Richmond. It was, above all, the continuing presence of a royal home that caused Richmond to develop from a village into a flourishing resort town.

Another factor was of course the pleasant situation beside the river and below the hill, and the clean air close to London. That factor itself influenced the continuance of the royal presence; and it was to bring in succession courtiers, nobles, rich merchants, the fashionable world and men and women of arts and letters to establish houses in the area. Three hundred years ago there was a spate of development projects and speculative building. Later, when the railway provided a new cheap and fast means of transport into and out of London, the middle classes moved from the metropolis to the burgeoning suburb, and the day-trippers flocked out to enjoy the amenities.

Catering for the visitor, whether courtier or diplomat, summer resident or day-tripper, has for centuries been one of Richmond's main industries, as its 'Wells', its succession of theatres, its very numerous pubs and inns, bear witness. Richmond has always been a prosperous place: its prosperity also attracted the poor – but its poor were on the whole well cared for, and such slums as developed were soon cleared away.

This book aims to tell, primarily in pictures, the story of Richmond from the time in 1501 when Henry VII retitled his newly rebuilt palace after the name of his Yorkshire earldom to the latest completed redevelopment project by the Richmond riverside. There is much that cannot be covered in detail in a short accompanying text. For that the reader – and the author – must turn to weightier volumes.

The Royal Founders

The manor of Shene was first separated from Kingston when Henry I granted it to the important Norman family of Belet. For nearly two hundred years Shene remained in lay hands, but at the beginning of the fourteenth century it reverted to royal ownership. King Edward II founded a house of Carmelite Friars in the manor house, but moved them to Oxford two years later. Shene then became the property of Queen Isabella who held it until her death in 1358.

It was after his mother's death that Edward III first converted the manor house into a royal palace – in which he died in 1377. His successor, his young grandson Richard II of Bordeaux, brought his teenage Queen, Anne of Bohemia, to Shene and it quickly became their favourite home. When Anne died there, suddenly, of the plague on Whit Sunday 1394 Richard was so heart-broken that he ordered the demolition of the first Shene Palace.

The second palace was the creation of Henry V and Henry VI. At the beginning of his reign Henry V set out to restore Shene. First, he moved to an adjacent site by the riverside the half-timbered manor house from Byfleet and its ancillary buildings, to create a complex that was known as 'Byfleet at Shene'. He then started work on a new main palace building – on a site between 'Byfleet' and that of the old palace – but this was not completed until the 1450s.

At the same time as starting work on the palace, Henry V resolved to found three new monasteries in the area. One foundation was abortive; the second was the Brigittine convent of Syon on the Middlesex side of the river. The third was the great Carthusian monastery (or Charterhouse) of Jesus of Bethlehem of Shene. Its site lay in what is now the course of the Royal Mid-Surrey Golf Club, in the Old Deer Park. It was by the river, just to the south-west of the later King's Observatory.

The Shene Charterhouse was the largest and the richest of all the pre-Reformation Carthusian houses in England. It flourished under continued royal patronage (Henry VII was a particular patron) until the dissolution. It was one of the few English monasteries, and the only Carthusian one, to be restored when Queen Mary I reconciled her country with Rome – but was rapidly dissolved again after the accession of Elizabeth.

1. *The death of Anne of Bohemia at Shene Palace*, (from a copy of *Froissart's Chronicles*).

2. *King Henry V*. (From an engraving by Greatbach of the picture at the National Portrait Gallery. Artist unknown.)

3. A model of the Shene Charterhouse as it was about 1450. (The model, in the Museum of Richmond, was designed by John Cloake and built by Scale-Link Ltd. It was sponsored by Solaglas Ltd whose office in the King's Observatory adjoins the site.)

King Henry VII recovered Shene Palace from Edward IV's widow (to whom it had been granted) in 1486. It was on 23 December 1497, when the King, his family and the court were at Shene for Christmas, that a disastrous fire broke out which destroyed or damaged much of the old building. King Henry, who had already started a programme of restoration and new works at the palace, now decided to rebuild completely – using however much of the old foundations and plan, and possibly even surviving parts of the fabric. When the new building was more or less complete, and ready for occupation, in 1501, he decreed that it should from thenceforth be known as his Palace and Manor of Richmond, rather than Shene. The village quickly also adopted the new name.

Henry VII's Richmond Palace was, for a while, the show-place of the kingdom. Towards the riverside stood the square stone building containing the royal apartments, with a central court and adorned with many towers (a relic of the fifteenth century plan, but lit by many and large windows), with a plethora of pepperpot domes capped with weather vanes and surrounded with King's beasts and pinnacles with more weather vanes. To the north of this building, and separated from it by the old moat, now crossed by a fixed bridge, was a larger court,

4. *Henry VII*, (an engraving from *Vestiges of Old London*, 1851).

with a fountain in the centre and flanked by the new great hall and chapel. The Middle Gate building, adorned with two figures of trumpeters, led through to the great main court, surrounded by brick buildings, to house court officials and the palace wardrobe, and with the outer gateway to Richmond Green. The wall fronting the Green was also adorned with squat towers and the range of lodgings extended behind it for most of its length.

On the western side of the Great Hall and the Fountain Court stretched the kitchens and domestic quarters of the palace, dominated by the great pyramidal roof of the Livery Kitchen. Between the old moat and the river, on this side of the palace, the site of Edward III's building had become the Great Orchard.

The privy gardens lay on the eastern side of the palace buildings, and a new and remarkable feature was the gallery which enclosed them, running all the way from the moat by the royal lodgings (which was later spanned by another bridge) round the perimeter until it turned back westward by the open tennis court at the corner of the Green and what is now Friars Lane. Two storeys in height, the gallery was open at garden level, enclosed on the upper storey, with big windows overlooking the gardens and tennis court. It provided a place for walking in all weathers, for playing and watching games, for admiring from the upper level the 'knots' of planted herbs and small hedges and the King's beasts which adorned the gardens.

Outside the gallery the King gave the old 'Byfleet' buildings to found a house of Observant Franciscan friars, dissolved in 1534.

Various additions and alterations were made to the palace in the succeeding century and a half. Most of the elaborate work on the turrets had to be taken down for it became dangerous, but the pepperpot domes remained; and otherwise there is not a great deal of difference to be seen between Wyngaerde's drawings of 1562 and Hollar's engraving three-quarters of a century later.

Henry VII used Richmond a lot, and died within the palace he had built. Henry VIII used it frequently in his early years as king. In or about 1525, however, Cardinal Wolsey made over to the King the even more splendid palace he had built nearby at Hampton Court. For the next five years, until Wolsey's fall, King and Cardinal seem to have shared the use of both palaces; but as the King began to distance himself from Catherine of Aragon and to instal Anne Boleyn in the Queen's place at

5. Two views of Richmond Palace drawn by Antonis van Wyngaerde in 1561–62. (Above): the north-east side from the Green. (Below): the south-west side from the River Thames.

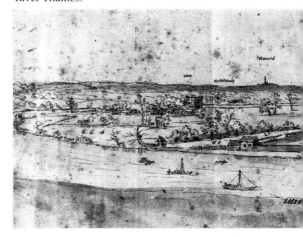

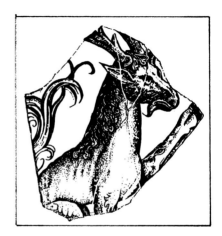

6. A fragment of painted glass from Richmond Palace, now in the Museum of Richmond (drawing by Caroline Church).

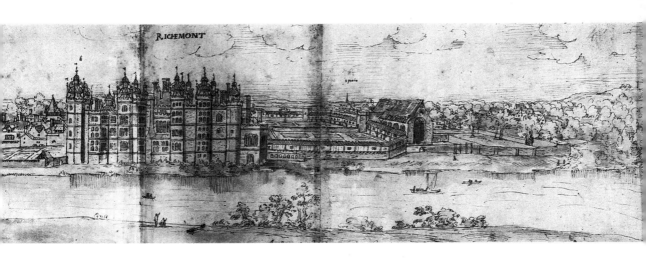

7. *Richmond Palace* in 1638 (engraved from a drawing by Wenceslaus Hollar).

8. *Richmond Palace and the ferry place, c*1620. (An engraving of 1774 by R.B. Godfrey from a painting now in the Fitzwilliam Museum, Cambridge.)

court, Richmond began to be spoken of as 'the Queen's palace'. After her mother's death and Anne Boleyn's execution, Richmond was used by Henry's eldest daughter Princess Mary. It was at Hampton Court that the future Edward VI was born, but at Richmond that his mother Jane Seymour died ten days later.

When the King's fourth marriage ended in a rapid divorce, Richmond was given to the rejected Anne of Cleves, who returned it, after Henry's death, to the young Edward VI. Queen Mary and Queen Elizabeth both used Richmond frequently. The Tudor court was always peripatetic, moving from one palace to the next after a stay of a few weeks – as much for sanitary reasons as any other. But Richmond usually saw the royal court in residence two or three times a year – and sometimes for longer periods if there was plague in London. The defence against the Armada was planned at Richmond. Many foreign ambassadors and suitors visited Queen Elizabeth there, and not a few treaties bore, at least ephemerally, the style of 'Treaty of Richmond'. In her old age Elizabeth preferred Richmond as a winter retreat – perhaps the relative compactness of the royal apartments there made it easier to keep warm. It was at Richmond that she died on 24 March 1603.

COURTIERS AT KEW AND SHEEN PLACE

The tiny hamlet of Kew had grown up opposite Brentford at the point where a ferry had replaced the early great ford across the Thames. It consisted of no more than half a dozen cottages until, at the beginning of the sixteenth century, Kew became the home of some of the leading courtiers. First was Charles Somerset, a cousin of Henry VII and commander of his guard, later Chamberlain of the household, who was created Earl of Worcester by Henry VIII. Then came the Earls of Devon, one of whom married Henry VII's sister-in-law and had a son who was advanced by Henry VIII to the rank of Marquess of Exeter, but who fell foul of Thomas Cromwell. Henry VII's daughter Mary, the widowed Queen of France, married Charles Brandon, Duke of Suffolk, and they first rented, then purchased, one of Somerset's houses at Kew. In another house at Kew lived first Henry VIII's friend, Henry Norris, accused of adultery and executed with Anne Boleyn; and later Edward Seymour, brother of Queen Jane. Most of these properties came at the beginning of Elizabeth's reign into the hands of Robert Dudley, her favourite whom she was to create Earl of Leicester.

Dudley had been married in 1550 at Sheen Place, the mansion formed out of the dissolved Charterhouse. At first on its dissolution it had been granted to Edward Seymour, who became Duke of Somerset and Lord Protector when his nephew Edward VI came to the throne. After Somerset's fall it was given to Henry Grey, Duke of Suffolk, whose wife was the daughter of Charles Brandon and Mary Tudor. With the Duke of Northumberland, who now owned Syon across the river from Sheen Place, he plotted to put his daughter Lady Jane Grey – Henry VII's great-granddaughter – on the throne instead of the Catholic Princess Mary when the sickly young Edward VI died. In Queen Elizabeth's reign, Sheen became the home of Sir Richard Sackville and his son Thomas, Lord Buckhurst, later Lord Treasurer and Earl of Dorset, and then of Sir Thomas Gorges and his Swedish-born wife Helena, Marchioness of Northampton, the widow of Queen Elizabeth's 'uncle' William Parr, and first lady of Elizabeth's court.

9. *Edward Seymour, Duke of Somerset*, (engraving by R. Cooper from the painting by Holbein).

10. *Robert Dudley, Earl of Leicester*, (engraving from *Vestiges of Old London*, 1851).

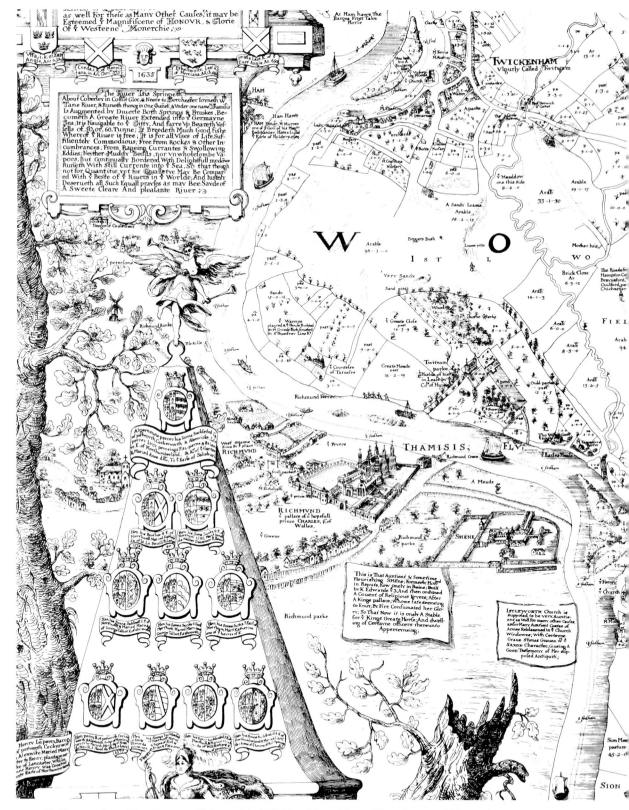

11. The area from Ham House to Richmond in 1635 (detail from Moses Glover's map of Isleworth Hundred at Syon House, Isleworth).

The Stuarts at Richmond

THE EARLY PARKS

When King James I came to the English throne in 1603 he almost at once set about creating a new park at Richmond. It was already the fourth royal park in the area. The original one attached to Shene manor house, which became Edward III's palace, was probably quite small, as most of the hunting took place in the open 'warren' between Shene and Kew. It seems likely that this park was split up and developed in or before Henry V's time, part of it perhaps being the site of 'Byfleet'. Henry VI had made 'the New Park of Shene', as it was called, to the west of the palace and the Green, between the river and the Charterhouse.

Henry VII, finding the New Park of Shene inadequate in size, created a new larger park facing the palace on the Middlesex bank of the river. As this was an appendage of the palace it was often called 'The New Park of Richmond in County Middlesex' – but less confusingly it also had the name of Isleworth Park. Queen Elizabeth granted it to Edward Bacon (whose brother Francis renamed it Twickenham Park), so James I was left only with the small 'New Park of Shene' – too small to indulge his passion for hunting. To this nucleus he added the former lands of the Charterhouse (but not the monastic site itself which he left to Sir Thomas Gorges), all that remained of the royal hunting warren and, as an afterthought, some 35 acres of land which he purchased from the holders of strips in the Richmond Lower Field. This gave him a park of some 370 acres, in the centre of which was built a hunting lodge. Sir Thomas Gorges, in compensation for the Charterhouse land he had given up, was made Keeper of this 'New Park of Richmond', and was given a 40-year lease of the manors of Ham and Petersham.

12. *Plan of King James I's New Park at Richmond*, 1605.

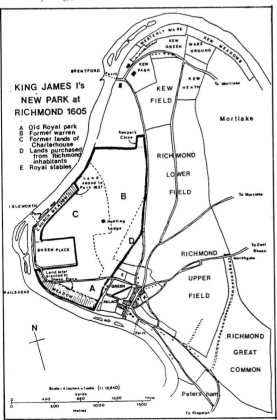

13. *James I*, (oil painting by Paul van Somer, 1571–1621).

14. *Henry, Prince of Wales* at Richmond Palace (portrait by Robert Peake, *c*1610, now in the National Portrait Gallery, London).

15. Design for a giant figure on a rocky mound with grottoes, by Solomon de Caux, intended for Richmond Palace (from de Caux's *Les Raisons des Forces Mouvantes*).

HENRY, PRINCE OF WALES

King James used Richmond Palace occasionally as an overnight stop with good hunting, but he soon decided to make it the country seat of his heir, Henry, Prince of Wales. From 1610 Prince Henry had his own establishment and court at Richmond. Very much a man of the Renaissance, Henry had wide interests and grand designs. He was an amateur of art and started to collect pictures and sculptures; he was an avid horseman (though he did not share his father's love of hunting) and built new stables and a riding school at Sheen Place which he rented from the widowed Marchioness of Northampton.

Henry intended to build a new palace at Richmond in the Italian style and brought in an Italian architect to plan it. He intended to lay out new gardens with giant statues and grottoes and waterworks and got the French landscape gardener Solomon de Caux working on the designs. To the young Inigo Jones, the Prince's Surveyor, fell the more mundane task of reclaiming a stretch of the river bank outside the Palace. It was probably as part of these works that the old moats were filled in about 1610.

Then suddenly Prince Henry died in 1612 at the age of twenty. All the new work came to an abrupt end; and when his brother Charles, the new Prince of Wales, was granted Richmond some five years later, he was content to leave it much as he had found it – only continuing and expanding Henry's art collection. As King, Charles granted the manors of Richmond, Petersham and Ham to his Queen, Henrietta Maria; and again Richmond Palace became a royal nursery. The young Prince Charles (the future Charles II) and his brothers and sisters spent much time there with their tutors and governesses.

16. Design for a fountain for Richmond Palace, by Solomon de Caux (from de Caux's *La Perspective*).

17. *Ham House* from the garden (painting by Hendrik Danckerts, now at Ham House).

18. A party in the grounds of Ham House, showing the front of the house facing the river (drawing by Thomas Rowlandson, now at Ham House).

HAM HOUSE

One of the leading figures of Prince Henry's court, Sir Arthur Gorges, seaman and poet, had acquired the former Somerset house and park at Kew. Another, Sir Robert Carr, later Earl of Ancrum, held the mansion and lands at Kew which had belonged to Robert Dudley. A third, Sir Thomas Vavasour, set out to build himself a new mansion by the riverside south-west of Richmond, on the borders of Petersham and Ham, which (though actually in Petersham) was called Ham House. Built in 1610, Ham House still stands, little altered externally, and with its gardens now restored to their seventeenth century layout.

In 1633 Ham House was purchased by William Murray, a close associate of King Charles I, for whom he had formerly acted as 'whipping boy' (being the nephew of one of Charles's tutors). After the outbreak of the Civil War Murray was created Earl of Dysart by Charles; he died in exile leaving no sons. On the Restoration his eldest daughter Elizabeth was recognised as Countess of Dysart in her own right. She married twice: first Sir Lionel Tollemache whose descendants inherited the house and the Dysart title; and second John Maitland, Earl and later Duke of Lauderdale – one of Charles II's favourites, and a member of the famous 'Cabal' of ministers. The interior of Ham House has been furnished according to an inventory dating from the time of the Lauderdales.

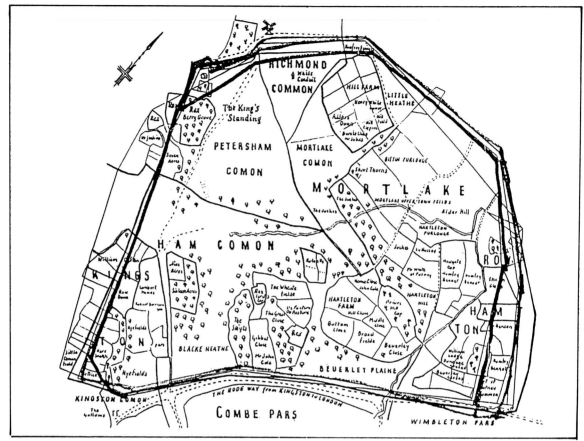

19. The formation of Charles I's new Great Park of Richmond (a modern redrawing of the original plan, on which several alternative boundary lines were marked).

KING CHARLES'S PARK

The great legacy of King Charles I to Richmond was his new Great Park – the present Richmond Park. But at the time of its formation it brought him much unpopularity. Although James I's 'New Park' was available to him, as was Hampton Court with its two parks, he wanted something much larger and more spacious. Conveniently close to Richmond Palace, at the top of the hill, lay a large open stretch of common land, divided between the royal manors of Richmond, Petersham and Ham, the town of Kingston, and the manor of Wimbledon (which included Mortlake, Roehampton and Putney) belonging to Edward Cecil, Viscount Wimbledon. The boundaries of this common land were, however, tortuous, and moreover there were within it some large closes of private land. To achieve a compact and unified park of the size and shape he wanted he decided that he would also have to acquire not only these private estates but also privately owned land in Mortlake and Roehampton including quite a lot

of the Mortlake common fields, and also some private holdings in Kingston and Petersham. By so doing he drew his boundaries so as to leave some small areas of common land for all the affected localities.

Though his advisers did their best to dissuade him, the King was determined to press ahead with his project. In December 1634 he set up a Commission to negotiate with the landowners and inhabitants over the necessary purchases. By April 1635 – although only five acres had by then been actually purchased – he had already started on the work of enclosure of the entire area by a high brick wall.

By 1637 most of the private landowners had been induced to come to terms – the compensatory payments were indeed very generous – and agreements had been reached with Viscount Wimbledon, with Gregory Cole (who held the manors of Ham and Petersham under a lease from Queen Henrietta Maria) and with the burgesses of Kingston about the enclosure of the common lands. It was, how-

20. *A staghunt in Richmond Park, c1640*, probably showing Ludovick Carlile, Deputy Keeper of the Park (painting by Joan Carlile, now at Lamport Hall).

ever, a matter of forced purchase: either one accepted the payment or one's land was enclosed without payment (as the vestrymen of Mortlake discovered when they held out too long over agreeing to part with some land recently donated for the repair of the church, for which they were still seeking compensation in 1676).

Mortlake was the hardest hit of the several communities affected, by the loss of part of their common fields as well as private estates and common land. The individual landowner who lost the most land was Gregory Cole of Petersham who had to give up not only his own house in Petersham but also his 220-acre Hartleton farm in the south-east part of Ham Common. Cole left Petersham, selling his leasehold interest in the manors of Petersham and Ham to William Murray of Ham House, and his two main houses were now to become the headquarters of the two deputy keepers of the New Park. The Earl of Portland, who owned Putney Park, and who had helped with the negotiations in Roehampton, was appointed Keeper or Ranger. Petersham Lodge, the former Cole residence, was allotted to Ludovick Carlile, whose wife Joan, an artist of distinction, painted a hunting scene in the new park. The Hartleton farmhouse was allotted to the other deputy keeper, Humphrey Rogers.

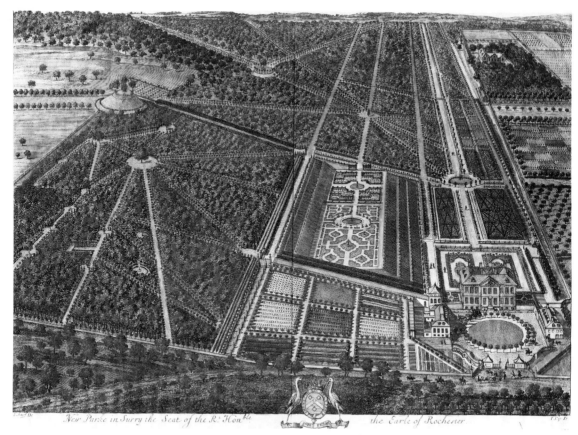

21. *'New Parke in Surry the Seat of the Rt. Honble the Earle of Rochester'* (engraving by I. Kip, 1708, from a drawing by Leonard Knyff). The old house at Sudbrook can be seen in the background on the right.

When Parliament sold off the royal estates after the execution of Charles I, Richmond New Park was not sold, but was given to the City of London. The Mayor and Corporation returned it to Charles II on his restoration, and he gave the keepership of the Park to Sir Lionel Tollemache and his wife the Countess of Dysart, and after Tollemache's death to the Duke of Lauderdale. When the latter died in 1683 the Countess surrendered her rights, and the keepership, together with Petersham Lodge, was granted to Lawrence Hyde, Earl of Rochester. Hyde obtained a personal lease of over 50 acres of the Park and had the lodge rebuilt as a splendid mansion, which he called simply 'New Park'.

THE DESTRUCTION OF RICHMOND PALACE

The sales by Parliament in 1649–50 included King James's park (by then known as the 'Little' or 'Old Park' of Richmond), Sheen Place (the former Charterhouse), the Palace itself, with the lordship of the manor of Richmond, and the lordships of the manors of Petersham and Ham.

The purchasers of the Palace, a syndicate, appear to have divided the property into a number of lots. The manorial rights and the ranges of brick buildings facing the Green were acquired by Sir Gregory Norton, one of the 'regicides' who had signed the King's death warrant. Title to the stone buildings – the chapel, the hall and the royal apartments – and to the tennis court, galleries and privy gardens seems to have gone to one Henry Carter. Instead of residing in this splendid mansion he used it as a stone quarry. He was later denounced as 'the first puller-down of the King's house'.

The process of demolition started almost immediately. In 1651 the manor court prosecuted a Richmond inhabitant for 'driving his cart loaden with stones...from the Great House cross Richmond Green out of the usual way'. By 1660 there was nothing left but the lodgings in the outer wall, the buildings around the Great Court including the

wardrobe and the Middle Gate, and some of the kitchen and domestic buildings. The first new building on the site was a house built in the 1650s by Carter on the site of the former tennis court (later enlarged to become 'Tudor Place').

After the Restoration the Gatehouse and the range facing the Green were occupied by Colonel Edward Villiers, Steward and then, by lease from Henrietta Maria, Lord of the Manor. The manor and Palace were then granted to the Duke of York, the future James II. Villiers' wife was appointed governess to the Duke's children and the Princesses Mary and Anne, both future queens, and other children were raised there. The other surviving buildings in the main court west of the gate and in the old kitchen complex were divided into separate dwellings, leased out by the Crown.

In the first decade of the eighteenth century, the old Middle Gate was replaced by Trumpeters' House, built for the diplomat Richard Hill by John Yeomans in 1702–04; and new houses (Old Court House and Wentworth House) were built on the site of the old lodgings west of the main gate. In 1724–25 a large part of the range facing the Green was pulled down to build Maids of Honour Row as residences for the ladies-in-waiting of Princess Caroline of Wales.

22. The front of Richmond Palace in the 1690s (drawing by F. Gasselin, now in the Museum of Richmond). The house on the far left is the one built in the 1650s on the site of the old tennis court.

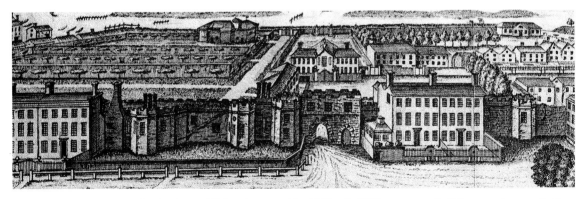

23. In W. Shaftoe's drawing of Richmond Palace (engraved by N. Parr in 1742) many new buildings can be seen. In the centre, behind the gateway, is Trumpeters' House. To the right are Old Court House and Wentworth House and behind them a row of houses converted from the former domestic and kitchen buildings of the Palace. On the far left is the end of Maids of Honour Row. By the riverside is the Earl of Cholmondeley's new library (not yet flanked by the mansion he built a few years later) and in the background on the far right is the brewhouse which occupied the site of the later Asgill House.

Village to Town

MERCHANT INVESTORS

It was from about 1690 onwards that Richmond began to develop from a village into a small but prosperous town. The main impetus appears to have been London money: rich merchants seeking both investments and summer houses outside, but conveniently close to, the capital. In some cases they rented existing houses – then, perhaps, bought and rebuilt them. John Knapp, a member of the Haberdashers' Company and of the 'Company of Merchant Adventurers Trading in the North West Part of America', first rented, then granted a mortgage on, then purchased outright, a house in the Marshgate (now Sheen) Road. Once it was his own property in 1699, he rebuilt it as 'Marshgate House' and proudly inserted his crest in the fine wrought-iron gate.

Other merchants bought land, and by purchasing and exchanging contiguous strips in the fields, built up small estates. Nathaniel Rawlins, another Haberdasher, consolidated an estate of some three acres at the western end of the Church Shot (on which some cottages had already been built) between Red Lion Street and the Vineyard. In 1696 he built for himself what is now Clarence House at the Vineyard end of the property; then he demolished one of the older houses and built in its stead a pair of semi-detached houses, back-to-back, each of four storeys.'The Rosary' and 'The Hollies', to give them their nineteenth-century names, must be almost unique as a pair of semi-detached houses of this size at such an early date. They were probably intended for Rawlins's two daughters (who both married, so never lived in them).

Rawlins invested in a lot of other property in the town. Some of his purchases were older houses and shops, but he also bought some newly-built houses, which he may have helped to finance.

24. Marshgate House, Sheen Road.

25. Clarence House, The Vineyard.

26. The Rosary and The Hollies, Ormond Road.

27. The Richmond riverside and the ferry from the Town Wharf, a painting of *c*1740 by Peter Andrew Rysbraeck, now in the Old Town Hall, Richmond.

28. The Riverside development project of the 1690s, shown in a detail from an engraving of 1755 after an earlier (?*c*1720) painting attributed to Tillemans. The two large houses in the centre were later known as Hotham House and Heron House. The one on the right was rebuilt in the 1820s.

Two major speculative developments were financed by rich Londoners who already had property in Richmond. John Saunders, 'citizen and merchant', acquired by marriage a house at the top of Ferry Hill. He then bought up a lot of adjoining property, and started to redevelop the site with three large houses facing the river, with access from a new court (Herring, later Heron, Court), and five smaller houses facing Hill Street. He died in 1694 before the project was completed, but his widow promptly remarried and raised a mortgage from her new husband to pay for completion of the work.

Among the tenants of these new houses were rich Jewish merchants. Readmitted into the country as recently as 1656, the leaders of the Jewish community in London were seeking to find a place in society. This was easier in the more relaxed atmosphere of Richmond than in London – and they flocked to rent houses there for summer occupation. John Mackay, writing in 1714, said that Richmond 'is the ordinary Summer Residence of the richest Jews, some of whom have pleasant Seats here.' The earliest surviving rate books substantiate this, by the number of Portuguese and Spanish names that they contain. A little later Jewish names from Germany and the Netherlands also become common.

29. Old Palace Terrace, Old Palace Place and Old Friars in the 1690s (detail from the Gasselin drawing, the rest of which is shown on p21).

Another project was financed by Virtue Radford, son of the Rev. William Radford, who kept a school in Richmond from 1661 until his death in 1673. Virtue Radford, an attorney (and son-in-law of the Lord Chief Justice), in 1688 purchased for his own occupation a large old house, formed from three late sixteenth- or early-seventeenth-century cottages which had been knocked together, facing the Green at the end of King Street. In the following year he bought the old mansion almost opposite. William Wollins, a local builder, was employed to demolish the old mansion and build in its place in 1692 a terrace of seven houses facing the Green (now Old Palace Terrace) and behind them a row of seven shops (the south-east side of Paved Court). It was probably Wollins who also built a new front, just one room deep, for Radford's own house (now Old Palace Place), leaving the backs of the old half-timbered houses behind it.

30. Old Palace Terrace, Oak House, Old Palace Place and a part of Old Friars in the snow in the 1930s.

31. The house on the left with the cornice is No. 12–14 Brewer's Lane, built by John Drew *c*1690.

32. *A view of Richmond from the Terrace*, painting by Leonard Knyff, *c*1720, now on loan to the Museum of Richmond from the Ionides Collection at Orleans House, Twickenham.

33. *A view of Richmond from the top of the Hill* in the 1630s (aquatint *c*1810 from an original drawing by Wenceslaus Hollar in the Queen's collection at Windsor). The Palace can be seen in the distance; the cottages on the right are on the same site as the houses in the Knyff painting above.

THE 'ARCHITECT' BUILDERS

Some of the master-builders of Richmond, whose original trades were carpenter, bricklayer or mason, saw the opportunity and began to anticipate the demand by financing new construction themselves. They began to figure in the manor rolls with a new description: 'architect'. A typical example was Michael Pew, son of a Kew brewer. In the late 1690s he bought up a little group of cottages on the top of Richmond Hill and replaced them with three large houses (Nos 1, 2 and 3 The Terrace), mortgaging each in turn to raise funds for the next, until he could sell the finished property. Whether or not he was also responsible for the original layout of the terrace walk, created about this time, is uncertain. Pew built other houses in Kew, and a large house in Old Palace Lane.

John Drew, descendant of a long line of Richmond bricklayers, by a similar technique, bought, mortgaged, and rebuilt for sale many properties in Richmond, including three of those purchased by Nathaniel Rawlins. One of his houses survives, little changed, in Brewer's Lane.

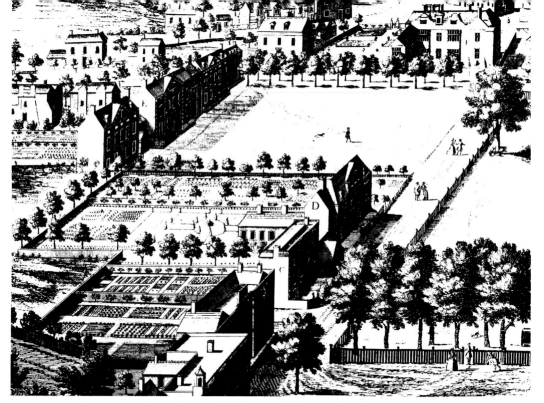

34. John Price's developments at the north-east end of Richmond Green and Little Green (detail from *The Prospect of Richmond*, 1726). The Jacobean mansion (top right) was the home of William Duke, from whom Duke Street derives its name, and later of the Michel family.

The most important of Richmond's 'architects' at this period, and the only one to enjoy more than a purely local reputation, was John Price. His major project in Richmond, which he financed himself through mortgages, was the development of the north-east sides of Richmond Green and Little Green. Here he built, between 1710 and 1725, six large mansions for rent to the nobility and the very rich, as well as two smaller houses facing Little Green (which still survive).

Price's tenants included the Marquess of Hertford, the Earl of Scarborough and the East India merchant Elihu Yale (benefactor of Richmond's parochial school as well as Yale University). Sadly, all Price's larger houses have long since been demolished; but among the other work in Richmond which can be attributed to him is No. 17 The Green, which was for much of the eighteenth century Richmond's leading coffee house.

Quite a number of substantial houses in the centre of Richmond, whose architects are unknown, survive from this period. In addition to those on the Palace site, they include the recently restored No. 5 Hill Street (date uncertain), Old Friars (refronted *c*1700), Nos 10–12 The Green (between 1705 and 1715), Lissoy and Nos 3–7 Ormond Road (probably 1700–10), the original part of Halford House (*c*1710), Vineyard House (*c*1720), 22 The Green (1724), and Nos 1–5 Church Terrace (*c*1725).

35. The south side of Richmond Green, a drawing by Thomas Way, 1900. Nos. 10–12 are on the left. The house in the centre, with a pediment, is No. 17, built by John Price, and Richmond's principal coffee house in the eighteenth century.

There were other master-craftsmen in Richmond who contributed their skills to the houses of this period: some of these buildings have very richly carved cornices and door frames. A particular artist, unidentified so far, was 'the master of the cherub heads'. He may have been John Vernon (1657–1730) who is named as a woodcarver in the parish registers, as is his son Francis Vernon (1685–1725). Eight doorheads of houses dating from 1690–1725 have one or two cherub heads, mostly similar in execution, incorporated in the corbels or the hood. A splendid overdoor carving (*c*1700) of a death and resurrection motif, which for 150 years stood over the west door of Richmond church, may be by the same hand.

Plumbers also provided richly decorated pump and rain-water spouts and cisterns. A good collection of the spouts is in the Museum of Richmond; the cisterns are known only through old photographs.

37. Doorhead of No. 3 Michel's Terrace, Kew Foot Road.

36. Lead cistern dated 1715 from No. 11 The Green.

38. Doorhead at No. 11 The Green.

39. Lead cistern dated 1755 from No. 22. The Green. It was used as an ash-bin in 1900 when the photo was taken.

40. *Petersham Lodge*, built in 1732 for the Earl of Harrington, in replacement of 'New Park' (engraving of 1752 from a drawing by Augustin Heckel).

BUILDING ON THE OUTSKIRTS

The end of the seventeenth century and the first part of the eighteenth also saw the building of some mansions on the outskirts of Richmond, along the Marshgate (now Sheen) Road, and in Petersham and Ham. Many of these were for the nobility and gentry. Carrington Lodge in the Marshgate Road was built for Sir Charles Littleton, Spring Grove at Marshgate for the Marquess of Lothian.

At Petersham, the Earl of Rochester's 'New Park' was joined in the late seventeenth century by Petersham House, Rutland Lodge, Montrose House (built for Sir Thomas Janner), and Douglas House (c1700). In 1726–28 the Duke of Argyll employed James Gibbs to rebuild the old mansion he had purchased at Sudbrook. After the destruction of 'New Park' by fire in 1721, a new house named Petersham Lodge was built for Lord Harrington by the Earl of Burlington in 1732. In Ham, Ormeley Lodge, Hardwicke House, Selby House, Beaufort House and Ham Manor House all survive from this period.

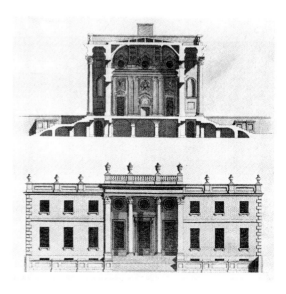

41. *Sudbrook House*, designed by James Gibbs for the Earl of Argyll (engraving from Gibbs's *Book of Architecture*, 1728).

42. *Richmond Lodge*, c1710 (detail from a painting of Syon House by Jan Griffier, *now at Syon House*). The central part only of the new south front had been added by this time, but not yet the wings. The stable block and the original riverside terrace were also completed.

Richmond Lodge and Gardens

The only work that Christopher Wren carried out at Richmond was some decoration and minor repairs of the Palace for James II in 1688, work which was stopped when the King went into exile. William III ignored the remains of the old Palace, but rediscovered the hunting lodge in the Old Park. He came for a day's hunting in 1693, stayed in James I's lodge, liked the place, and had repairs put in hand. Two years later, after another, longer visit, he ordered the enlargement of the house and improvement of the gardens, including the creation of a broad avenue from the house to the riverside. Much of the park land had been let off for farming, and this was now gathered together again into the hands of the King's friend, John Latten, who was made Steward of the Manor and was given a lease of the lodge and park.

After King William's death, Latten sold his lease to James Butler, Duke of Ormonde, a distinguished soldier, Lord Lieutenant of Ireland, and formerly married to the Queen's cousin. Ormonde was granted a new lease for 99 years, rented additional land at the Kew end of the park, and set about making further improvements and additions to the house, rebuilding its south-east front completely, and further adorning the grounds with a riverside terrace and summer house.

Ormonde, who succeeded the Duke of Marlborough as Commander-in-Chief in 1712, was very popular in the whole country – and particularly in Richmond, where a tavern and a new row of houses were given his name. But he was a staunch Jacobite. He went into exile in France in the summer of 1715, participated in the attempted invasion and rebellion that autumn; and all his estates were forfeited. A lien on Richmond Lodge, however, had been assigned in 1712 to his brother the Earl of Arran, who was able to secure the release of the property, which he then leased to the new Prince of Wales. In 1718 Prince George and Princess Caroline moved into Richmond Lodge.

Richmond was to remain a favourite country resort of George and Caroline until the latter's death in 1737. Further additions were made to the house, but it remained too small and Caroline rented addi-

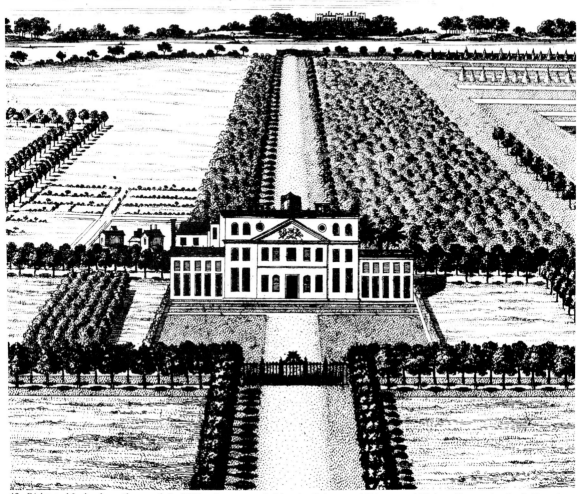

43. *Richmond Lodge* from the south in 1725, when occupied by the Prince and Princess of Wales. (Engraving by I. Van de Gucht – the foreground has been cropped.)

tional houses at Kew (including the present Kew Palace), as well as having Maids of Honour Row built in Richmond for her ladies-in-waiting. Her main interest however was in the grounds and in 1727, when George (now King George II) settled the Richmond property on her, she engaged Charles Bridgeman to remodel the whole of the northern end of the estate. She also bought and demolished houses on Richmond Green and in the Kew Foot Lane to make new entrances into the Park.

The terrace walk by the riverside was extended up to Kew, a canal was made, and new planting and paths in 'the Wilderness'. A 'dairy-house' was built

at the end of the canal, and William Kent designed for her a stone grotto called 'The Hermitage' and a curious building with thatched beehive-like domes called 'Merlin's Cave'. The Hermitage was decorated inside with busts of philosophers, Merlin's Cave with waxwork figures of legendary characters.

After Caroline's death, the King suspended all further work on the gardens, but he continued to make use of the Lodge, bringing his mistress, Lady Yarmouth, and a small party of friends to dine there 'every Saturday in summer', as Horace Walpole tells us.

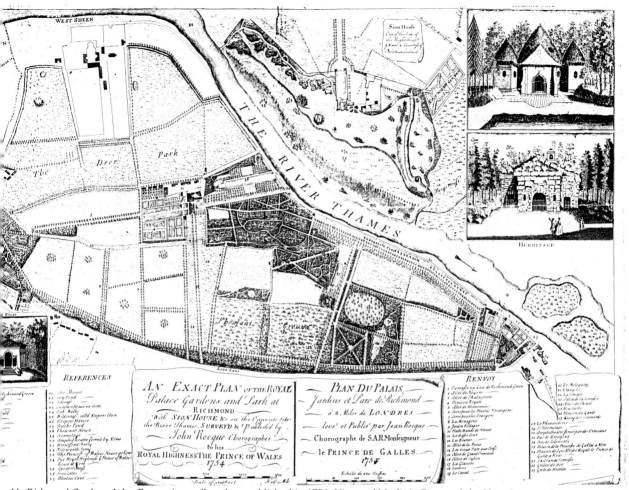

44. *Richmond Gardens.* John Rocque's smaller plan, published in 1754. Views of Merlin's Cave and the Hermitage are inset at top right; at bottom left is the Dairy House built at the end of the ornamental canal.

George III inherited the Lodge from his grandfather in 1760, and immediately after his marriage in 1761 took his bride to visit Richmond. From 1764 until 1772 they spent part of every summer there. Launcelot 'Capability' Brown was engaged to redo the gardens – and he swept away the works of Bridgeman and Kent.

The King was not, however, content with Richmond Lodge and almost immediately embarked on the idea of replacing it with a new Richmond Palace (an idea with which George II and Caroline also toyed, commissioning plans from the Irish architect Edward Lovett Pearce and from William Kent). Now it was the turn of William Chambers, who had been working on George's mother's estate at Kew. He eventually prepared at least four plans, and work based on the third of these actually started in 1770. To improve the views all the houses of 'West

Sheen' were bought back and demolished. First, however, the King, a keen astronomer, had Chambers build an observatory. This was in 1769, to enable the King to watch the transit of Venus across the sun in June of that year. In 1770 the Queen had a thatched cottage built as a tea-house in the woods to the north of the old Lodge, and near to it established a menagerie.

Work on the new palace proceeded slowly, for the King was paying for it out of his own pocket, already depleted by the purchase of Buckingham House in London. When his mother died in 1772 he moved to her house at Kew, and work at Richmond stopped altogether. The grand plans were abandoned and Richmond Lodge was demolished that same year, the foundations of the new palace a few years later.

45. *'The Prospect of Richmond in Surry'*, published by Overton and Hoole in 1726.

46. *'A View of Richmond, looking towards Twickenham'* by William Marlow. On the left is the mansion built by Edward Collins, later rebuilt and called Lansdowne House. On the right can be seen the boundary fence of the Wells, and the 'Mews House'.

Fashionable Richmond

THE PROSPECT OF RICHMOND

The Prospect of Richmond, published in 1726, gives a good general impression of the town in the early eighteenth century. There are some glaring errors of topography: the omission of a lot of land by the riverside from the ferry down to the Palace site and the convergence into one of Richmond Hill and the Petersham Road are two of the most obvious. Hill Street is greatly elongated and Red Lion Street, Ormond Road and the Vineyard are confused, as are the Kew Horse Road and the Kew Foot Road; and part of the south side of the Green is missing. Nevertheless, the details of the buildings that have survived or that can be compared with other pictures are in most cases quite accurately depicted. One can easily distinguish (by gables and fenestration) earlier seventeenth-century buildings, such as the Red Lyon Inn, the Castle Inn and Mr Michel's house at the corner of the Green and Duke Street, from those that had been built within the last thirty to forty years.

RICHMOND WELLS

The development of Richmond as a summer resort created a need for entertainment. A big boost was given in the 1670s by the discovery on the hillside of a chalybeate spring, with waters having some of the qualities of those of Epsom. The spring was at first exploited just as a medicinal spa, but a new lease-holder in 1696 developed the area as pleasure gardens with a pump room, assembly and gaming rooms. Daily concerts and weekly balls became a regular feature.

For some fifty years Richmond Wells attracted the custom not only of residents and summer visitors, but also of Londoners. Advertisements showed the tide times for those arriving by river, while large stables and coachhouses were provided for those who preferred to risk the journey by coach. It is an extraordinary fact that no single illustration of the Wells has ever been identified. The picture here shows on the right hand side the boundary wall, and in the right middle distance the 'Mews House' and stables.

By the 1750s the Wells had been deserted by most of the fashionable world and was attracting instead a rowdy element, resented by inhabitants. Susanna Houblon, living almost opposite on the Hill, purchased the main buildings of the Wells in 1763, and closed them down.

THE EARLY THEATRES

The Wells provided musical entertainment, but there had been no theatrical performances at Richmond since the destruction of the royal Palace, where Queen Elizabeth had had regular short seasons of plays at Christmas and Shrove-tide, and where the Stuart princes had put on occasional masques.

The first recorded play at Richmond outside the Palace was staged in the summer of 1714 by the Earl of Southampton's Company, possibly at a barn on the Hill belonging to Nathaniel Rawlins. Four years later, the well-known comedian William Pinkethman may have used the same barn for a short theatrical season. In 1719 he opened a new theatre in a converted building of Scott's 'Royal Ass House' next door (the hiring out of donkeys both to ride and for transporting goods was a flourishing business).

Pinkethman's theatre died with him in 1725, but Thomas Chapman, an actor who had performed there, soon started another. This was purpose-built, on a rented site a little further up the hill (on the site of Nos 10–12 Richmond Hill). It was opened in June 1730, and Chapman continued to give a summer season of performances each year until his death in 1747. His widow remained as lessee for ten years, but about 1753–54 the building lost its licence for theatrical performances and became the 'Music Room'.

Theophilus Cibber tried in 1756 to get round the lack of a licence by advertising it as a warehouse where 'cephalic snuff' (i.e. wit) could be bought by patrons who might see, free of charge, 'rehearsals' by students of the drama school which just happened to use the same premises. It was a good try-on, but it did not last, for Cibber died in 1758. There was a brief revival of regular theatre in the 1760s, but in 1765 a new and larger theatre was opened on Richmond Green. The playhouse on the Hill struggled on against the competition for a year or two, but then sold out; for twenty years the building was used for a dissenters' meeting house, and later as a stable and store. It seems to have been demolished in the 1820s.

47. *Thomas Chapman's Playhouse* on Richmond Hill.

48. *Theophilus Cibber.*

TWO RICHMOND POETS

Stephen Duck already had a reputation as a rustic poet in Wiltshire before he came to Richmond Lodge as a protégé of Queen Caroline in 1730. When he married, as his second wife in 1733, Sarah Bigge, the housekeeper of the Queen's House at Kew, the *Gentleman's Magazine* referred to him as 'the famous thresher poet'. In 1735 the Queen appointed him as Keeper of Merlin's Cave and of her library there, where he continued after her death. He took holy orders in the mid–1740s and acted as chaplain to the Dragoons on guard duty at Richmond Lodge. He left Richmond to become Vicar of Byfleet in 1752 – and drowned in the Thames four years later.

James Thomson enjoyed great popularity in his day, especially as author of a long poetic cycle, *The Seasons*. A Scotsman, he came to London in 1725 at the age of twenty-four.'Winter' was published in 1726 and the other seasons followed in successive years. In 1736 he took a cottage in the Kew Foot Lane, where he worked at a revision of *The Seasons* and wrote other poems and a number of plays. His most famous composition, the ode 'Rule Britannia' in Dr Arne's *Masque of Alfred*, was published in 1740. He rose at noon, spent much time taking long walks, and not a little in drinking with his many friends. He died at his cottage in August 1748 and was buried in Richmond Church, but it was not until 1792 that a memorial plate was erected there at the expense of Lord Buchan. Though now almost forgotten, Thomson stands with the greatest, for his monument in Poets' Corner in Westminster Abbey is located next to that of Shakespeare.

50. *Stephen Duck* (from the frontispiece in his *Poems*).

51. The summerhouse in the garden of 'Rosedale' was believed to be where Thomson used to work (engraving 1831 from Cooke's *Views of Richmond*).

49. *James Thomson.*

The Old Churches

The first church in this area was probably that at Kingston, but by the time of the Domesday Survey in 1085 there was also one in the manor of Petersham, belonging to Chertsey Abbey. Soon after the great priory of Merton was founded in 1114 by Gilbert the Norman, a former Sheriff of Surrey, he gave the church at Kingston to the priory as an endowment. The original deed appears to have been lost by the early thirteenth century, but by that time, at least, there were four chapelries attached to Kingston church: the original church at Petersham, and new ones at Shene, Ditton and East Moulsey. The first mention of the 'parish of Shene' occurs in a document of 1220.

Of the original fabric of Petersham and Shene (now Richmond) churches nothing now remains, although the north wall of the chancel at Petersham contains some twelfth century work.

Both churches were largely rebuilt in the reign of Henry VII. St Peter's at Petersham, which was rebuilt in 1505, was very small, but it had a tower at the west end. By 1635 the tower had a spire. Some small transepts were probably added in the seventeenth century, and the north transept was enlarged either later in that century, or early in the eighteenth. The upper part of the tower was probably rebuilt at about the same time, as it had acquired its present shape, with the cupola replacing the spire, by 1720. Despite the urging of the curate, Mr Bellamy, in the 1770s and 80s that the church, then in considerable disrepair, should be enlarged or entirely rebuilt, nothing was done – except some structural repairs, and the remodelling of the interior in 1796 – until 1840 when the south transept was considerably enlarged, new galleries were built and other changes made, which almost doubled the seating.

The interior of Petersham church today retains the old box pews and galleries of 1840, and is little changed save for the installation of an organ. The pulpit dates from 1796; the reading and clerk's desks, now in the south transept, originally stood in front of it.

52. (top) St Mary Magdalene's Church, Richmond and 53. (middle) St Peter's, Petersham in 1635 (details from Moses Glover's map shown on p.14).

54. Petersham Church has kept its early nineteenth century interior, complete with box pews and galleries.

The rebuilding of the parish church of Richmond, dedicated to St Mary Magdelene, seems to have begun in the late 1480s, when a new tower was built, and to have continued during the next twenty years. In 1506 Henry VII contributed £10 towards the leading of the roof. A new south aisle was built at the expense of Sir George Wright *c*1614 and the top of the tower was rebuilt in 1624. At an uncertain date (but possibly 1703) a cupola was erected on the tower. A new north aisle and door were built (by John Price) in 1699, and then in 1750–52 the south aisle and the main body of the nave were rebuilt to the designs of Robert Morris, a native of Twickenham.

A major scheme of alterations was carried through in 1864–66. This involved little change to the exterior except for the removal of the cupola, the replacement of the north porch by a new one beside the tower, and the removal of the old dormer windows in the aisles. The interior was, however, entirely reconstructed. New galleries were built, bench pews replaced box pews, and the high pulpit (which dates from the 1699 enlargement) was separated from the reading desk and set on the four short legs it has today. A timber roof replaced the old plaster ceiling, and a lot of the monuments were moved around. The side galleries were finally taken down in 1903 and in the following year the old Tudor chancel was replaced by an entirely new east end (architect G.F. Bodley) containing chancel, a new chapel and a vestry. At this time the tower was resurfaced in flint, to match the new east end. The last major change came in 1935–36 with the removal of the west gallery.

The main artistic and historical interest in the church today is in its fine monuments, including a Tudor brass, three splendid Jacobean monuments with kneeling figures, sculptures by Flaxman and John Bacon, and memorials to writers and actors as well as to the gentry of Richmond.

Although Richmond had long operated virtually as a separate parish, its status remained officially that of a chapel within the Vicarage of Kingston until 1849, when Richmond (already then itself divided into two separate parishes) finally became a Vicarage in its own right. Petersham remained within Kingston until 1788 when it was united with Kew as a combined Vicarage.

55. *Richmond Parish Church* in 1726 (detail from *The Prospect of Richmond*).

56. The interior of Richmond Parish Church *c*1840 (engraved by James Darnill from a drawing by I. Shaw).

57. *Richmond Parish Church* from the south-east in 1807, showing the Tudor chancel (engraving by S. Woodburn).

ST ANNE'S CHURCH AT KEW

Until the early eighteenth century Kew residents either attended church at Richmond or went by ferry across the river, to Brentford. But in 1710, a group of the Kew gentry got together to build themselves a chapel. From Queen Anne they obtained a grant of land on Kew Green and a donation of £100, to add to what they had raised by subscription, and on 12 May 1714 the chapel was consecrated and dedicated to St Anne, as a chapel-of-ease to Kingston. This remained its status until 1769, when Kew and Petersham were united in a separate combined Vicarage – a step not formally put into effect however until 1788 when Mr Bellamy, who had been curate of both churches, died. Similarly an Act of 1850 to separate the Vicarages of Kew and Petersham did not become effective until 1891.

St Anne's, supported by royal patronage and a rising population, was frequently enlarged. In 1770 and again in 1805 George III paid for the work: new north and south aisles were built, and the west front was extended. In 1822–23 the east end was enlarged to house an organ presented by George IV, and in 1837 the west front was rebuilt by Sir Jeffrey Wyatville at the expense of William IV. The church was further extended eastwards in 1851 to provide a mausoleum for the Duke of Cambridge, and again in 1884 when the entire east end was rebuilt to the plans of Henry Stock. The vestry rooms on the north side were added in 1902 and the adjacent parish room in 1979.

58. *St Anne's chapel in Kew Green* in 1714, from the frontispiece of a printed Charity Sermon preached in 1721.

59. *St Anne's, Kew* from the south-west, after the alterations carried out by Robert Browne in 1805 (a watercolour in the Richmond Public Library).

60. *The White House at Kew* engraving from a drawing by W. Woollett, 1763).

The Palaces at Kew

Though Henry VII's daughter Mary had lived at Kew briefly with her husband the Duke of Suffolk, and James I's daughter Elizabeth lived there for some years before her marriage to the Elector Palatine, the long and continuous association of the royal family with Kew really began in 1728 when Queen Caroline rented Kew Farm and the 'Dutch House' and, within a year, three nearby houses. The Dutch House, so called from its architectural style being that of Flanders and the Netherlands, had been built in 1631 by a merchant, Samuel Fortrey, whose family originated from Lille in Flanders and whose wife was a native of Hainault. The Queen used all these houses to accommodate her children and household while she was using Richmond Lodge.

Three years after this expansion into Kew, her eldest son Frederick, Prince of Wales, acquired the lease of Kew Park. Already renowned for its gar-

dens when owned by Sir Henry Capell in the late seventeenth century, the mansion and its small park was now the property of Elizabeth Capell. Her first husband, Samuel Molyneux, who had been secretary to George II when Prince of Wales, was a keen astronomer and built an observatory in the east wing of the house.

Frederick employed William Kent as his architect to improve and enlarge the house which, when finished, was plastered on the exterior and became known as the 'White House'. This distinguished it from the red-brick Dutch House which faced it across a narrow strip at the end of Kew Green, then much longer than it is today.

As altered by Kent, the White House had an almost square central block of three storeys, with two single-storey wings added on the south front. The formal gardens were quite small, but Frederick

61. Frederick, Prince of Wales, with three of his sisters in the garden of the White House. The 'Dutch House' (the present Kew Palace) is in the background. (Painting by Philip Mercier, 1733).

and his wife Augusta began to develop an interest in botany, one which was encouraged by the Earl of Bute, himself a keen botanist. Frederick decided to expand and improve his grounds and to create a garden for exotic specimens. In 1749 and 1750 he purchased and leased an additional 42½ acres of land, extending the estate southwards to the driveway between Richmond Lodge and the Kew Road. He began work on an aqueduct, a lake and an artificial mount, installed a chinoiserie summer house – The House of Confucius – and planned to build a great new glasshouse for the exotic plants. But then, in March 1751, he died suddenly.

This time, unlike 1612, the death of the heir to the throne put only a temporary stop to great garden works. Princess Augusta continued them with the help of Bute, and to the designs of Chambers, appointed in 1757 as architectural tutor to her son George, the new Prince of Wales, and as architect to Augusta herself.

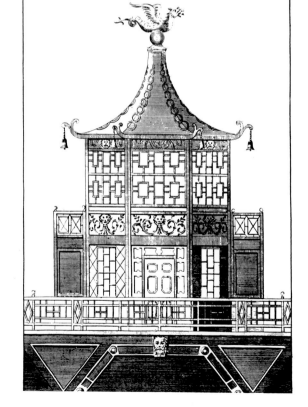

62. *The House of Confucius* (from the *Gentleman's Magazine*, 1773).

63. The Alhambra, the Pagoda and the Mosque in the gardens at Kew (engraving 1763).

Chambers planned the grounds as an enclosed essay in the 'natural' style, for Kew was very flat and there were no rolling hills to form a background. There were two great stretches of lawn, a large lake, and around the perimeter, thickly planted with trees, a winding walk, to be adorned with a plethora of classical temples, exotic buildings such as a 'mosque', an 'alhambra' and the great pagoda, a gothic 'cathedral', a ruined Roman arch and other such follies. Nearer to the house, to the east side of the lawn, was the classical orangery, the original botanical garden (of some nine acres), an aviary and a menagerie (with another Chinese building). By 1763 the layout was complete.

When Princess Augusta died in 1772, George III and Queen Charlotte moved from Richmond Lodge to the White House at Kew, which was enlarged for them by Chambers. The King then abandoned his plans for building a new Richmond Palace, and from 1776 Windsor began increasingly to find favour as a summer retreat. The royal couple however still visited Kew regularly, and the botanic gardens were further developed under the guidance of Sir Joseph Banks, who took over Bute's role as a general, but honorary, supervisor. Then, in 1788, the King was smitten with his first serious bout of what was then considered insanity, but is now diagnosed as porphyria. He was moved from Windsor to Kew for treatment and then convalescence. Thereafter, perhaps because the White House now held unpleasant memories for the royal couple, Windsor was clearly preferred to Kew.

64. *Augusta, Princess of Wales*, from a painting by Allan Ramsay, *c*1758.

65. The 'swan' on the lake at Kew was a boat, propelled by pedals, which could take ten passengers (engraving from a drawing by W. Woollett, 1763).

66. *The Temple of the Sun*, (engraving from a drawing by G.E. Papendiek *c*1830).

67. The Menagerie at Kew and, (on the left) the Temple of Bellona (engraving from a drawing by T. Sandby, 1763).

68. The 'Castellated Palace' at Kew built for George III by James Wyatt (engraving from a drawing by F. Nash, 1810).

At the end of the century the King's interest in building a new palace revived. In 1799 the Earl of Essex (from whom the White House was still rented) died, and the King purchased the estate. The other Kew houses, used by the children and household, had already been bought in 1781 and these, except the Dutch House, were now demolished to make way for a new palace, to be built by James Wyatt. This was to be a castle by the river, in the fashionable Gothic style, but it was a pioneer building, with the load carried on a cast-iron frame. It had a high, turretted, central 'keep', with office buildings disposed round a large courtyard.

As the plans developed the White House itself was demolished and the King and Queen used the Dutch House as a pied-à-terre at Kew when they came to check on progress. By 1805 the shell of the new building was complete, but the King was not only suffering more frequent attacks of madness, but was also becoming blind. He could no longer enjoy his new palace and work was almost completely suspended in 1806. From 1807 he was virtually confined to Windsor and never visited Kew again. Queen Charlotte came occasionally, and spent the last five months of her life at the Dutch House in 1818.

The great castle by the riverside was never occupied and George IV, who disliked it intensely, had it demolished in 1828.

69. *The remains of Kew Palace*: part of the stable block of the White House (engraving from a drawing by G.E. Papendiek *c*1830).

70. The first page of the deed of grant by George III and Queen Charlotte of the Richmond commons to the Vestry in 1786.

Local Government

Richmond's local government in the second half of the eighteenth century was closely linked to the history of the royal estates, for George III enjoyed his role as the local 'squire'. However, to understand that situation, it is necessary to look back at the earlier institutions.

In the Middle Ages, local government was a matter for the lord of the manor and his courts and, at a higher level, for the county sheriff and the county courts. The principal manorial court was the 'court baron', usually presided over by the lord's steward, with a jury or 'homage' made up of manorial tenants. This upheld the customs of the manor, which defined the rights of both lord and tenants, and also recorded the transfer of land and property. At the court the land was 'surrendered' back into the lord's hand and regranted to the new owner, subject to the payment of a fee. This transaction was registered in the court rolls and a copy of the entry served as title deeds. Land held on this basis was therefore called 'copyhold'. This court also supervised the maintenance of hedges, ditches and highways.

A second manorial court was the 'court leet' or 'view of frank pledge', originally a means of ensuring that all tenants had made their homage to the lord, and were duly inscribed for the payment of feudal dues and taxes. To the court leet belonged the duty of electing from among the manor tenants officers such as the constable, the headborough or tithing-man, and the ale-conner. The quality of local ale and the baking of bread was under its supervision as was the settlement of minor disputes.

Shene, later Richmond, had its court baron from the earliest times, but only acquired its own court leet in 1629, having previously been under that of Kingston. As both courts were thereafter held on the same days, with the same attendance, the boundaries of jurisdiction soon became blurred.

The other old established territorial division was the ecclesiastical parish. The development of the poor laws in the sixteenth century, finally codified in the great Act of 1601, had placed the parish in charge of poor relief, and had laid down rules for the appointment of overseers. From this beginning stemmed the development of the parish as a local government organisation. In Richmond, the old, unstructured, parish meeting was soon virtually replaced by an executive committee – the Select Vestry, the establishment of which was authorised by the Bishop of Winchester in 1614. This body consisted of the minister, the churchwardens and a group of the local gentry and leading citizens – self-appointed and self-perpetuating by co-option. The Vestry dealt with church matters, such as repairs to the fabric and the allocation of pews; it assessed, collected and, through the overseers, distributed the poor rate. In Richmond, during the Commonwealth period, it chose new ministers and, in 1651, raised a special rate to pave the roads leading from the Green to the Church (Brewer's Lane and Church Court). As the Vestry grew in importance, the manor courts tended increasingly to confine themselves to the business of manorial property, though exerting themselves to contest the usurpations of rights of way by those who bought the Palace in 1650.

By the second decade of the eighteenth century, however, the authority and energy of Richmond's Select Vestry seems to have begun to flag. It met less frequently and did little but approve the churchwardens' accounts. In its place, the Parish General Meeting, under the aegis of the churchwardens, began to assume greater importance. It was the General Meeting, not the Vestry, which dealt with the establishment of a workhouse in 1729, and in the following year the new watchhouse and fire-engine house. By 1749 the Select Vestry hardly met at all; on 3 April that year the Parish General Meeting changed its name to that of General Vestry, and on 3 December the Select Vestry held its last recorded meeting.

This democratic development, however, had its drawbacks. The powers of the General Vestry were undefined and dubious. The opportunity for reform presented itself in 1766. In that year George III wanted to close the old public road which ran along the riverbank from the Kew-Brentford ferry and then turned to cross the royal estate, only a few

71. *The Vestry Hall* built in Paradise Road in 1790 (from Somers Gascoyne's *Recollections of Richmond, c*1899).

hundred feet from Richmond Lodge, to reach Richmond Green. The road was less used since the building of a bridge at Kew in 1759 and in its place the King proposed not only to improve and extend the towpath, but also to widen and maintain in perpetuity the direct road from Kew Bridge to the Bear Inn at the outskirts of Richmond town. A deal was struck, and incorporated in an Act of Parliament which also tackled the question of Richmond's local government. The Vestry was in future to be confined to church matters. In its place there would be elected 'Parish Trustees', to whom were given powers to raise the poor and highway rates, to provide for the paving, lighting and watching of the streets, to enforce new rules about drainage from houses, and so on.

The Trustees under the Act of 1766 set to their tasks with a will. They drew up new orders for the conduct of the workhouse; they surveyed the unkempt nature of the streets and introduced regular street cleaning and a paving programme; they installed street lamps and established a night watch with specified beats. One of their first concerns was to ask the King for a grant of land on the common on which to build a new workhouse. He agreed to this subject to an approach being made through the manor court, but on this point, surprisingly, the Trustees failed to follow up. There may have been an element of jealousy of the continuing authority of the manor court, but the main problem was that they didn't know how they were going to finance the building of a new workhouse.

Another deal between King and inhabitants was struck in 1774, when Sheen Lane, the old road to the Charterhouse, was closed in return for improvements, at the King's expense, to the alternative route by Palace Lane and the riverside and the further extension of the towpath. But this had no local government spin-off.

In 1780, as the condition of the old leased workhouse was becoming acute, the Manor Steward prompted the Trustees to revert to the idea of a grant on the common – they might, perhaps, take over the old pesthouse built there, outside the park wall, in the second part of the seventeenth century. This time the Trustees did get the approval of the manor court, but they still delayed while they thrashed out the terms of a Bill to give themselves greater powers. By 1785 the Bill was presented to Parliament but then at the last minute was amended to allow for the closure of Love Lane, the old 'foot road' from the Green to Kew Ferry, for the entire length that divided the royal gardens of Richmond from those of Kew. Judging from the terms of the Trustees' petition, they were as keen to close this 'dangerous nuisance' as was the King himself.

The Bill was duly passed. The Trustees were replaced by a new, elected Vestry with the extra powers they had sought. In 1786 the King and Queen granted it the whole of Hill Common and almost all of Pesthouse Common – double the amount of land they had asked for. What was not needed for the workhouse and a new cemetery was to be held 'for the support and employment of the poor' – and so the Richmond Parish Lands Charity came into existence. The King built the new workhouse at his own expense. One of the first acts of the new Vestry was to build a Vestry Hall on Paradise Road, at the end of the new Vineyard Passage burial ground.

72. The Hill Common and the original terrace walk, detail from a painting by Leonard Knyff *c*1720. On the left are the Roebuck tavern and Nos 1–3 The Terrace, and beyond them the windmill. The Bull's Head tavern is at centre right.

THE RICHMOND COMMONS

Among the rights of manorial tenants were those of pasturing animals and gathering firewood on the waste and common land. Richmond's Great Common was on the slopes of the hill, stretching down to the river to the west, to the road to East Sheen to the north-east and to the meeting point with Petersham and Mortlake Commons to the south.

The first important encroachment on the Great Common took place even before the enclosure of Charles I's New Park. It was a grant of land in return for the provision of services to the community. In 1621 an acre of land at the top of the hill, by the corner of the Upper Field, was granted to Thomas Mercer on condition that he should build there a grist mill to grind the inhabitants' corn. The windmill stood (where the Richmond Gate Hotel is today) for a hundred years. From the 1670s further grants of land were made on the north side of the windmill until most of the land west of the lane down to Marshgate was in private hands.

After the enclosure of the Park, only a narrow neck of common was left between the windmill and the park gate. In 1639 this was further reduced by the granting out of land outside the park wall, which effectively divided the remaining common into two parts: one between the top of the hill and the Marsh Gate at the manor boundary on the road to East Sheen, and one on the slope of the hill towards the river. In the same year an acre strip of the latter along the boundary with Petersham Common was granted out on condition that the grantee should maintain a fence with gates and stiles – to prevent animals straying from one manor to another.

The Hill Common was further eroded in the late 1630s by grants of land on its northern side to tile makers. Richmond's original tile kilns had been set up between the Petersham Road and the river in the reign of Elizabeth, but the tile makers needed to dig clay out of the hillside. By 1646 an acre and a half of the Hill Common had been granted for this purpose, and new kilns were established at the foot of the hill, on the east side of the road.

So eagerly did the tile makers dig out clay, sometimes outside the land granted to them, that the manor records are full of complaints: that landslides were caused, that livestock was at risk and so on. The King put a stop to illegal digging in 1766 and a year later the tile kilns were closed down and the land sold to the Duke of Montagu, who turned it into a pleasure garden. When the King granted what remained of Hill Common to the Vestry in 1786 it was with the strict condition that no new building should be erected there.

73. *Richmond Windmill* as depicted in Moses Glover's map of 1635.

74. *The Richmond Workhouse* (from Somers Gascoyne's *Recollections of Richmond*, c1899).

THE RICHMOND WORKHOUSE

When the General Parish Meeting first decided in 1729 to set up a workhouse, they found temporary accommodation in a group of four cottages (probably behind the Orange Tree tavern). In the following year they took over the lease of a large seventeenth-century house called Rump Hall, in the Petersham Road. Within a few years all the poor who had been receiving regular pension payments which allowed them to reside in their own homes, were moved into the Workhouse, for which a Master and a Matron were appointed. This building was used until 1787 when the new one on Pesthouse Common was available, and was by then over-crowded, with other pensioners living outside it.

The new workhouse, designed by Kenton Couse (who had built one at Barnes a few years earlier) was a large, practical building with a central block and two wings. It did not stand exactly on the site of the old Pesthouse, for that was not demolished until later. To the main building, paid for by the King, the Vestry added an infirmary and a 'lunatic wing'. (Poor George III, when convalescing at Kew early in 1789 from his bout of madness, walked up to visit his workhouse, where the Master with more enthusiasm than tact insisted on showing him the lunatic wing, discoursing volubly on the use of strait-jackets. The King, who had recent experience of such restraints, took it all with complete composure.)

Though some of the land on Pesthouse Common was leased out, more than half of it was used as the Workhouse Farm, cultivated by the inmates, who also worked at spinning, weaving and leather work, producing clothing and shoes; able-bodied men were also employed on digging gravel and road repairs and some were recruited for the night watch. Richmond looked after its poor well, if quite strictly. The food was good, and attempts were made to teach not only the children but also some of the adults. Children, when they reached the appropriate age, were apprenticed or put to domestic service locally. In 1834 Richmond's administration of its poor was held up as an example to the country.

However, the new Poor Law Act of 1834 removed the Workhouse from parish control. It became a Union Workhouse under a Board of Guardians, serving a wider area. In 1913 it was renamed the 'Poor Law Institution' and when workhouses were abolished in 1948, it became the Kingsmead Old People's Home, which continued until 1974. It has now been converted into luxury flats.

The Almshouses

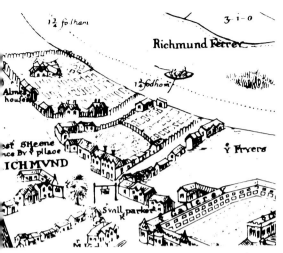

75. The first Richmond almshouses can be seen in this detail from Moses Glover's map of 1635.

76. *Queen Elizabeth's Almshouses* as rebuilt in 1857 (from Beresford Chancellor's *History and Antiquities of Richmond, etc*, 1894).

Official poor relief was supplemented by private charity. Many people left bequests for the poor in their wills; sometimes these were single gifts of money or food; sometimes they endowed an annual distribution of food, clothing, fuel or pensions. Most generous of all was the endowment of almshouses. Richmond's prosperity is reflected in the very large provision of almshouses in the town.

The first were founded in 1600 by Sir George Wright. They housed eight poor aged women, and were built beside the Petersham Road, some hundred yards south of the end of Ferry Hill. Sir George's father-in-law, Sir Robert Wright, increased the endowment. At first they were just called 'the Almshouses', and later 'the Lower Almshouses', but when a third foundation was established near them, the name of 'Queen Elizabeth's Almshouses' was gradually adopted. Why the Wrights were not given the credit they deserved is a continuing puzzle.

By 1767 the Almshouses were in a decayed state and had to be rebuilt. William Turner of The Hermitage in Church Terrace gave a plot of land at the southern end of his grounds, by the lane leading to the Vineyard, as a site for a new building funded by public subscription. No picture exists of these. They were rebuilt two more times, in 1857 and in 1955.

77. *Queen Elizabeth's Almshouses* today.

The second foundation was that by Brian Duppa, Bishop of Winchester, in 1661. Duppa had been a tutor to Charles, Prince of Wales (the future Charles II), and had remained with his charge at Richmond Palace, although appointed successively to the sees of Chichester and of Salisbury, until the outbreak of the Civil War. Deprived by Parliament of the bishopric of Salisbury because of his royalist connections, he lived throughout the Commonwealth period in a house in Richmond, on the site of the Town Hall building, which had been purchased for him by his friend Sir Justinian Isham. A whole nest of royalist sympathisers lived in that area of Richmond, and on at least one occasion Duppa's house was raided and searched, but he was not arrested.

Duppa was made Bishop of Winchester at the Restoration, but kept his Richmond house, at it was within his diocese. He died there in 1662, visited by the King on his deathbed. It is said that years before

he had vowed to found almshouses if his erstwhile pupil were to be restored to the throne, and in 1661 he bought land at Sunbury and Shepperton to endow almshouses at Richmond for ten unmarried women over 50 years of age. These were built on the Hill, facing Hill Common, at the corner of the lane leading to the Friar's Stile. And there they remained until 1852, when they had decayed to the point at which rebuilding was necessary. The owner of Downe House, the adjoining property, took the opportunity to extend his grounds. In a deal with the almshouse trustees, he provided a new site in the Vineyard adjacent to Queen Elizabeth's Almshouses, and offered to pay for the rebuilding himself in return for the old site, which he turned into a kitchen garden. (It later became the site of Downe Terrace, now Stuart Court.)

The almshouses were rebuilt in the Vineyard in a 'Jacobean' style by the architect Thomas Little. The old gateway and commemorative tablet were brought down from the hilltop site and re-erected.

78. The original building of Duppa's Almshouses on Richmond Hill (detail from the Knyff painting of *c*1720 on p25.

79. Architect's sketch of the proposed new building for Duppa's Almshouses in 1852.

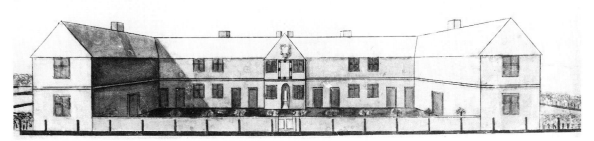

80. *Michel's Almshouses* as originally built (from a drawing by John Pullen made in 1716).

So far Richmond's almshouses provided only for women. In 1695 Humphrey Michel (who lived in the mansion at the corner of the Green and Duke Street – William Duke had been his stepfather) redressed the balance by founding almshouses for ten men, married or single. These were built in the lane leading to the Vineyard on part of 2½ acres of land which he gave as an endowment together with property in London. He died, aged 83, in the following year, but his nephew and heir, John Michel, completed the building and increased the endowment. Michel's Almshouses were rebuilt in 1811; and then in 1858 a further six were constructed in a row at right angles to the main building, backing onto Lancaster Road.

In 1759 Rebecca Houblon, the spinster daughter of a former Governor of the Bank of England, who lived with her sister in the mansion on the rise of the Hill which is now Old Vicarage School, founded almshouses for nine single women. These were located on land she owned by the Marshgate (now Sheen) Road, where the old Worple Way diverges from the line of the later road. They consisted of three blocks around a square enclosed garden. After Rebecca's death her sister Susanna continued her work. These almshouses have never been completely rebuilt, and are therefore the oldest ones now standing in Richmond.

81. *Michel's Almshouses* today, showing on the right the new wing built in 1858.

82. *Houblon's Almshouses* today.

83. *The Church Estate Almshouses, c1900.*

Two nineteenth-century foundations were not individual benefactions but built by trustees of existing charities. William Hickey of Richmond had, by his will in 1727, founded a trust which provided pensions for six men and ten women. This was endowed with property in Richmond which became increasingly valuable and the trustees, with an excess of funds, built almshouses. They purchased land at the far end of Marshgate Road and in 1834 engaged the architect Lewis Vulliamy to erect twenty almshouses (ten each for men and women), with a chapel and gate lodge cottages for a porter and a nurse. Hickey's Almshouses have been expanding ever since – twenty-nine units have been added over the years.

84. *Hickey's Almshouses, c1900.*

The Trustees of the Church Estates also found themselves with an excess of funds and pursued the same course. Ten almshouses for men and women were erected in 1844, to the plans of W.C. Stow, on a site adjoining that of the Hickey Almshouses; in 1968 another eight were built behind the original row.

85. The three original Petersham almshouses can be seen in the centre foreground of this engraving of Augustin Heckel's view from the top of Richmond Hill looking down-river, published in 1752.

Petersham had a single almshouse foundation. Three houses were built on the slopes of Petersham Common in 1729 but some thirty years after the building of Wick House its owner complained of the state of the almshouses and the smell of the pigs kept by the occupants. It was agreed to sell the site to him and in 1809 the proceeds of the sale were used to erect five almshouses at the bottom of the hill. They were rebuilt again in 1867 and demolished in 1953.

Ham's first almshouses were two cottages by the common gates, built from the proceeds of a sale of common land to the Duke of Argyll. Later, a group of four houses, funded from the 'poors' land', a strip of common by the Portsmouth Road which had been left out of Richmond Park, were built just off Ham Street. They have now been converted into a modern bungalow. The latest foundation in the area is Tollemache's Almshouses, further along Ham Street, founded in 1892 in memory of Algernon Gray Tollemache by his widow. They are for three couples and three single persons.

86. The Petersham almshouses and the back of the Star and Garter Hotel in an early photograph (c1860).

87. *Tollemache's Almshouses* at Ham.

88. *The Richmond Ferry* (drawing by James Marris *c*1770).

Crossing the River

The earliest crossing point of the River Thames in the vicinity of Richmond was the great ford at Brentford, which may have been used by the invading Romans, and was certainly utilised by English armies fighting the Danes in 1016, when Edmund Ironside won a battle on the Surrey side of the ford. The building of a bridge at Kingston in the twelfth century reduced the importance of the ford.

The precise date at which a regular ferry was established at Shene is unknown. The earliest reference to it is January 1443 when John Yong was appointed 'keeper of the boat and ferry over the Thames at Shene Manor' in succession to Thomas Tyler. In 1479/80 Richard Scopeham was granted the ferry and all tolls, 'provided that nothing be taken for the conveyance of the King's household'. From the early sixteenth century grants of the ferry rights, clearly a valuable asset, run in a continuous record; the usual recipients were crown servants or gentry, who had to provide the boats and employ the ferrymen. In the mid-seventeenth century there were two boats at Richmond ferry, one for carts and carriages, the other for horses and foot passengers.

At Kew the ferry seems to have been left to the enterprise of Brentford watermen until 1536 when Henry VIII granted a monopoly of the 'Cao ferry' to John Hale – an act which aroused protest from Brentford. A disaster was noted in October 1579 when John Dee of Mortlake recorded in his diary that after four days of continuous heavy rain 'the fote bote for the ferry at Kew was drowned and six persons by the negligens of the ferryman overwhelming the bote upon the roap set there to help, by reason of the vehement and high water.'

A competitive ferry was set up in 1659 by Robert Tunstall, who owned lime kilns in Brentford, half a mile down river. Although its primary purpose was to transport lime across the river, he advertised it for general purposes, and when challenged in the courts maintained that the old ferry (which still had its monopoly) was dangerous, inefficient and far too expensive.

Another ferry, for foot passengers only, was established between the north side of the Charterhouse site and Isleworth by the mid-sixteenth century.

Kew bridge joining the precedent

89. *The first Kew Bridge* (from a sketch by de Leutherbourg).

THE FIRST KEW BRIDGE

The first bridge over the stretch of Thames between Putney and Kingston was a wooden one, built at Kew in 1759. Its builder was Robert Tunstall, proprietor of the ferry, a descendant of his namesake of a hundred years earlier. His original plan was to erect it by Lot's Ait but it was thought this would interfere with the operations of barges, and so he moved the site. The bridge, designed by John Barnard, had eleven arches, four of stone and seven of timber, the central arch having a 50-foot span.

90. James Paine's design for Richmond Bridge. (The tollhouse at the Twickenham end, on the right, was omitted when the bridge was built.)

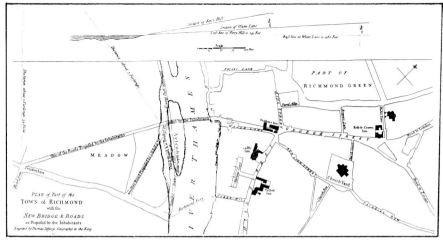

91. The inhabitants' proposal for a bridge situated at the end of Water Lane. The sections at the top show the approach slopes at the Ferry Hill and Water Lane sites. (Plan by Thomas Jefferys, 1773.)

RICHMOND BRIDGE

Pressure now grew for a bridge at Richmond as well. William Windham, owner of the ferry, first suggested a timber bridge in 1760, but failed to get permission. Although in the meantime he had sub-let his ferry grant to Henry Holland, he revived his proposal in 1772, but he was opposed by Holland whose financial interest was threatened, and by many inhabitants, who wanted a bridge but not the narrow timber one on masonry piers, on the line of the ferry crossing, that Windham was proposing. Ferry Hill, they argued, was steep and awkward for carriages. The residents, led by Henry Hobart, produced a counter-proposal for a stone bridge on the line of the main street approached down the gentler slope of Water Lane. This excellent scheme required, however, a new access road on the Twickenham side and the owner of the land there refused permission.

In the end a compromise was reached. The bridge would have to be on the Ferry Hill site, but the access would be improved and the bridge would be made entirely of stone. The interests of Windham and Holland were bought out, Bridge Commissioners were appointed in 1773, and a design by James Paine and Kenton Couse was adopted. In August 1774 Henry Hobart laid the first stone.

Construction was financed by two issues of tontine shares – a system by which the total interest payable was divided between the surviving holders of non-transferable shares, until the last one died. The bridge was opened to pedestrians in September 1776 and to vehicles in January 1777, and it was finally completed by December that year. The tolls levied were the same as those for the old ferry, and these were abolished in March 1859 after the death of the last surviving holder of the first issue of shares.

In 1937, after the new Twickenham Bridge had been opened, Richmond Bridge was widened. The upstream side was carefully demolished stone by stone, and replaced exactly as before after the piers had been lengthened and the arches and roadway widened.

92. *Richmond Bridge under construction* in 1776 (engraving by V. Green and F. Jukes after a painting by W. Hodges).

93. A sketch of Richmond Bridge by Thomas Rowlandson, showing the tollhouse at the Richmond end.

94. A watercolour of the second Kew Bridge by J.M.W. Turner.

THE SECOND AND THIRD KEW BRIDGES

The original bridge at Kew was not a great success. In 1774 it was damaged by a collision and remained closed for two years. More repairs were needed in 1782 and Robert Tunstall, son of the original builder, decided to get James Paine, whose Richmond Bridge had been acclaimed as a most elegant structure, to design a new stone bridge for Kew, to be built on the eastern side of the timber one. This bridge, of nine main arches, was begun in 1783 and completed in September 1789 when George III led 'a great concourse of carriages' across it.

This new bridge had been financed, like Richmond's, by tontine shares. In 1873 it was sold to the Metropolitan Board of Works and the tolls were abolished. When its widening was considered in the 1890s, it was found that the piers were too weak and that rebuilding would be safer and more economical. The structure we see today, designed by Sir John Wolfe Barry, was begun in 1899 and opened by Edward VII on 20 May 1903.

95. The present Kew Bridge, shortly after its opening in 1903.

96. *The railway bridge at Richmond*, 1848 (lithograph).

THE RAILWAY BRIDGES

As related below (see pp 70–71), the railway reached Richmond from Nine Elms in 1846. Two years later the London and South Western Railway began to extend the line, first through Twickenham and Staines to Datchet and then in 1849 to Windsor. This involved carrying the new line over the Thames by the first railway bridge across the river in the London area. This was designed by the company's own engineer, Joseph Locke, and had three 100-foot spans made of cast-iron ribs, with stone-faced piers, approached on the Surrey side by a brick viaduct of seven arches. It was opened in August 1848. The superstructure was replaced with steel arches in 1908, but its original appearance was retained.

The railway bridge at Kew was opened in 1869 as part of the new link built by the LSWR to connect with the North London Line and, in 1877, with the District Railway. It was designed by W.R. Galbraith and has five river spans with cast-iron cylinder piers.

97. A view of the river through the main land arch of the railway bridge (painting by George Hilditch).

98. *Richmond lock and weir* and the two footbridges, a photograph from the programme for the opening ceremony in 1894.

RICHMOND LOCK AND WEIR

Since the rebuilding of London Bridge in 1832 had removed the old obstructions which operated as a weir, the tides had risen and fallen far more quickly and the river at Richmond was often reduced to a muddy narrow stream. Many proposals for dealing with the problem were discussed, but eventually in 1890 the building of a new lock and weir was authorised. The superstructure required for the operation of the sluices was elaborated into two parallel footbridges, each of two onshore spans and three river spans, of steel and cast-iron. The lock and footbridges were opened by the Duke and Duchess of York on 19 May 1894.

The Late Eighteenth Century

The second half of the eighteenth century, and particularly the decade of the 1770s, saw another surge of development in Richmond. Many large villas and mansions were built, along the river, on the slopes and crest of the Hill, and along the Marshgate Road, some smaller houses around Kew Green, and cottages in the lanes and alleys around the centre of Richmond.

One of the first of the new generation of riverside villas was that built about 1760 by the architect Sir Robert Taylor for Sir Charles Asgill, Lord Mayor of London in 1757–58. Though much altered in the nineteenth century, Asgill House happily survived to be restored to its original elegance in 1970.

At about the same time, at the southern end of the Richmond riverside, by the boundary with Petersham, the Earl of Cardigan (later Duke of Montagu) built a new mansion in 1761–63. This was later inherited by Montagu's daughter, the Duchess of Buccleuch, and acquired the name of Buccleuch House. The Duke of Montagu extended his grounds along the riverside and then, after purchasing the tile kiln grounds and converting them into gardens, linked his two properties by a tunnel grotto under the Petersham Road.

Other new riverside houses were Bath (later Northumberland) House (1766), Bellevue (enlarged in the 1770s), Ivy Hall (c1757) and Bingham House (c1771).

99. *Asgill House*, a watercolour by Thomas Rowlandson.

100. *Buccleuch House* on the occasion of a fête in honour of the Queen's visit to the Duke of Buccleuch on 23 June 1842 (engraving by T.A. Prior from a painting by T. Allom).

101. The riverside at Richmond from the Castle Hotel to Camborne (later Northumberland) House (above) and from there to the Paragon (below). Two views from Samuel Leigh's *Panorama of the Thames from London to Richmond*, published c1830.

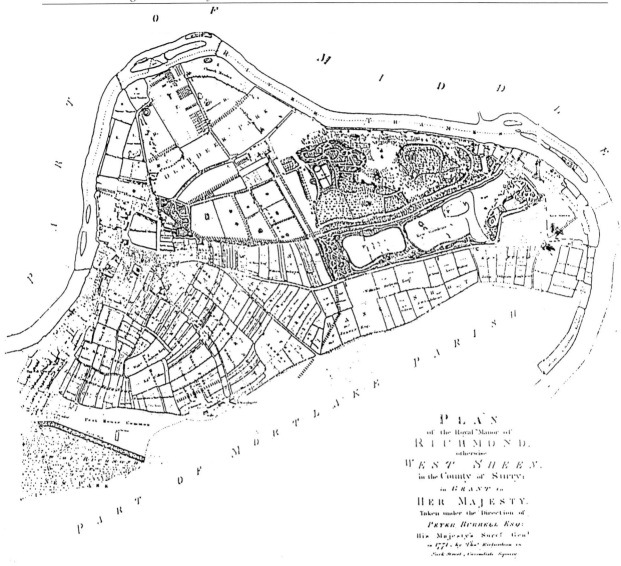

102. *Plan of the Manor of Richmond 1771*. A major new survey was made in 1771 of the entire manor. Every building and parcel of land was accurately mapped on detailed large-scale plans, and was numbered. Acreages and details of ownership were recorded. Several single-sheet maps were also made, to various scales, reproducing the detail from the large-scale plans.

The 1770s were the scene of great building activity on the top of the Hill. No. 3 The Terrace was rebuilt in 1769, and Doughty House considerably enlarged at about the same date. In 1771 Downe House was built for Charles Pearce, and Sir William Chambers started to build Wick House for Sir Joshua Reynolds. A new block was added to the old Star and Garter tavern, and opposite it the Duke of Ancaster bought up the houses outside the park wall and replaced them by a new mansion, Ancaster House, in 1772.

The Hickey Trustees, who owned the group of ramshackle wooden cottages which constituted the Bull's Head tavern, decided that the time had come to improve this property and in 1774 offered the site on a new building lease. It was purchased by Lady St Aubyn, who employed Robert Mylne to design the elegant villa called The Wick. The rebuilding provided the opportunity to extend the terrace walk up to the Star and Garter along the top of Petersham Common, and the road up the Hill was paved up to the Star and Garter corner.

Two new mansions were also built a little lower down the Hill. In 1765 Edward Collins, the brewer, built a house opposite the end of Friar's Stile Road which, enlarged in 1770, and then rebuilt in 1796, became a seat of nobility. Its successive occupants in the century from 1770 were Viscount Molyneux (later Earl of Sefton), Lady Di Beauclerk, George Townshend Earl of Leicester (later Marquess Townshend), the Marquess of Stafford, the Marquess Wellesley, the Marquess of Lansdowne and the Prince de Joinville.

Below it, on a site formerly occupied by a part of the Wells buildings, Robert Mylne built a house in 1791–93 for Mr Robert Sayer, which the latter promptly let to the Duke of Clarence. It was subsequently owned by the 5th and 6th Earls of Cardigan, from whom it took the name by which it was known until its demolition in 1970. (These two houses are illustrated on page 123.)

103. *The Wick and Wick House*, with the Star and Garter Inn, the park gates and Ancaster House in the background (watercolour by J.I. Richards, *c*1800).

104. *Richmond Hill*, an engraving published in 1782 from a drawing by Henry William Bunbury.

THE LASS OF RICHMOND HILL

The Terrace and the top of Petersham Common became a favourite place for promenades and for admiring the view – painted and engraved innumerable times and commended in verse and in prose. The fashionable world flocked up Richmond Hill to be drawn by Rowlandson and Henry Bunbury (a Richmond inhabitant); and the song, *The Lass of Richmond Hill*, first sung at Vauxhall Gardens in 1789, became a popular hit. The words are by Leonard MacNally and the music by James Hook.

Many theories have been advanced as to the identity of the lass – from Maria Fitzherbert (who dwelled not on Richmond Hill but in Marble Hill, Twickenham) to a Miss Cropp, who threw herself from an upper window of the house which is now part of the Richmond Hill Hotel when her father forbade her lover, a penniless lieutenant, to see her again. For many years it was the accepted truth that the song in fact referred to Richmond in Yorkshire and that the lass was Frances I'Anson of that town (who married Leonard MacNally). Recent research by Leslie Wenham, historian of Richmond, Yorkshire, has however shown that there is no basis for this belief.

There was probably no particular lass – but it remains a very good song.

THE LASS OF RICHMOND HILL.

On Richmond Hill there lives a lass
More bright than May-day morn,
Whose charms all other maids surpass—
A rose without a thorn.

This lass so neat, with smiles so sweet,
Has won my right good-will;
I'd crowns resign to call her mine,
Sweet lass of Richmond Hill.

105. *The Lass of Richmond Hill*, a nineteenth-century song sheet.

THE GOTHIC STYLE IN RICHMOND

While Richmond produced no building of the Gothic style to match the detail and perfection of Horace Walpole's Strawberry Hill, it was clearly influenced by its neighbour across the river. George III's great 'castle' at Kew has already been shown on p. 44, and the outstanding Gothic building of the Wesleyan Institution is considered later, as are the nineteenth century churches.

On a smaller scale, Richmond still has a Gothic castle. The late seventeenth century mansion on the Hill, which had been occupied by the Houblon family, was rented after the death of Susanna Houblon by Mrs Harriett Ellerker. In 1810 she purchased the house and had it completely altered externally with the addition of turrets and battlements. (It is now the Old Vicarage School.)

In the Petersham Road, by the riverside, Gothic House was built about 1810, incorporating in part an earlier house. One of its early occupants was Madame de Stael. Gothic House was demolished in 1938 when the road was widened.

A smaller – and much later – domestic gem is the cottage at the beginning of the Lower Mortlake Road, built in 1853. This was originally one of a pair. Its neighbour was sacrificed to the new roundabout in the 1930s.

106. *Ellerker House, Richmond Hill* (now the Old Vicarage School).

107. *Gothic House* in the Petersham Road – the front facing the river (demolished in 1938).

108. *Richmond Theatre* in 1804 (an aquatint by T. Woodfall from *The Theatric Tourist*).

THE THEATRE ROYAL

In 1765 a new and larger theatre was opened at the corner of Richmond Green, by the end of Old Palace Lane. The site, jutting out into the Green, had been occupied by a house for two hundred years. The new theatre was the initiative of James Dance, who used the stage name of James Love, encouraged by his friend David Garrick. It was not outwardly an imposing building, nor was it ornate internally, but it was planned with advice from the technical staff of Drury Lane, and described as 'a model for theatrical architects'. There was 'no convenience or accommodation which may not be found', including the ability to cover the pit and turn it rapidly into 'an elegant ballroom'.

The prologue on the opening night, 15 June 1765, was written by Garrick and spoken by Love. At the Theatre Royal, as it was called with good reason for it had frequent royal patronage, appeared such famous players as Dorothy Jordan, William Macready, Sarah Siddons, Edmund Kean and Helen Faucit. After frequent early changes of management it settled down for nearly twenty years under that of Charles Klanert. It was he who introduced Kean to Richmond where he first appeared in 1817. Kean

109. Interior of the Richmond Theatre, showing the last scene in *Richard III* (with Edmund Kean as Richard III). (An etching by F. Cornman, 1896.)

succeeded Klanert as actor-manager in 1831 and lived the last two years of his life in the house attached to the theatre. There was such a crowd at his funeral in Richmond Church that a friend exclaimed, 'Bravo, Ned, you've drawn a full house to the last!'

SOME RICHMOND CHARACTERS

JOHN CHRISTIAN BACH, youngest son of the great Johann Sebastian Bach, was known as 'the English Bach', for he settled in London in the 1750s and spent the rest of his life there – much of it as concert master to George III. He had a house at Richmond in the 1770s (though which has not been identified). Mrs Papendiek gives an account of how Bach and other court musicians practised quartets and quintets each week at her father's house on Kew Green. Each in turn had to introduce a new composition; and one evening Bach, having forgotten it was his turn, composed the first movement of a new quintet on the spot, with copyists writing down the parts looking over his shoulder as he worked them out.

SIR JOSHUA REYNOLDS, President of the Royal Academy and famous portrait painter, decided in 1771 to build a villa in Richmond. He acquired a grant of land at the top corner of Petersham Common from the Earl of Dysart, and asked Sir William Chambers to act as his architect. The house was originally intended just as a place to entertain friends, but as correspondence between Chambers and Reynolds reveals the latter changed his mind so often about his requirements that, although the house was a very simple one architecturally, the price had doubled by the time it was finished in 1772.

In it Reynolds did indeed entertain many of the leading figures of the day, and from it he painted his only important landscape – a view from Richmond Hill.

JUDITH LEVY was the daughter of the rich Jewish merchant Moses Hart, a leader of the Ashkenazi community in London. Hart rented a house in Herring Court from about 1710 to 1718, then moved to Isleworth. Judith Hart married her cousin Elias Levy, but was left a widow at an early age. From 1754 until just before her death in 1803 she lived at No. 4 Maids of Honour Row on Richmond Green. Extremely rich, eccentric, and at first very sociable, though later something of a recluse, she was renowned for good works, and earned her nickname as 'Queen of Richmond Green'. She paid most of the cost of rebuilding the Great Synagogue in Duke's Place, London, which had been built at her father's expense.

110. *John Christian Bach*, portrait by Thomas Gainsborough.

(Mrs JUDITH LEVY.)
The *Rich* Jewess *usually called*
The *Queen of Richmond Green*

111. *Mrs Judith Levy*, an engraving of 1803.

112. *The Princesse d'Hénin.*

113. *Jacques Mallet du Pan.*

THE FRENCH ÉMIGRÉS

Richmond became one of the centres of settlement for refugees from the French Revolution. The French nobility, though living in straitened circumstances, both kept up a social life of their own and participated in that of their English friends. The letters of Horace Walpole, Mary Berry and George Selwyn are full of references to them.'Mesdames de Biron and Cambis have taken houses on Richmond Green,' reported Walpole on 14 May 1790, 'as well as les Boufflers and Madame de Roncherolles.'

Three of the four members of a little clique of Princesses, friends from childhood, all settled in Richmond: the Princesse d'Hénin, the Princesse de Bouillon and the Duchesse de Biron. The Princesse d'Hénin, who escaped to England in 1792, rented the Rosary in Ormond Road. She shared this house with the Comte de Lally-Tollendal. Mme d'Hénin's niece wrote that 'their age should have guaranteed them from scandal, but they were nevertheless the butt of considerable ridicule.'

This niece, the young Marquise de la Tour du Pin, who wrote a famous and fascinating memoir of her exile in England and America, arrived in 1798 to stay with her aunt in Richmond. She later moved to a small house on, or just off, the Green. The Princesse de Bouillon was another arrival in 1798.

One of the more flamboyant members of the French community was the Comtesse de Balbi, mistress of the Comte de Provence (later Louis XVIII), who rented Reynolds's former residence, Wick House, on the Hill.

Some well known writers stayed briefly in Richmond. Chateaubriand spent part of the summer here in 1799; Madame de Stael lived with her last lover (and eventual husband) in Gothic House in 1813–15. Another was the Swiss-born historian and journalist Jacques Mallet du Pan – a refugee from Napoleon rather than the Revolution. His was one of the families that remained permanently in England, and has produced several distinguished British diplomats. He is one of the many French refugees buried in the Vineyard Passage burial ground.

Many other refugees' names appear in the local records, of both aristocrats and commoners. Not all were diehard royalists and reactionaries. Lally-Tollendal had been hailed as 'the Cicero of France' when he was a member of the Constituent Assembly. The three Princesses were all free-thinkers and constitutionalists.

The Coming of Steam

The age of steam locomotion first appeared in Richmond in 1816 – on the river. A river steamer was an appropriate beginning, for until well into the eighteenth century travel to Richmond from London had usually been by water. The bad roads, the highwaymen, the need, anyway, to take a ferry from the north bank, made the river preferable. And even when new bridges were built, (Putney was first in 1729), there were still plenty of watermen, with regular tariffs, to row passengers up and down, or across, the river. Their fare from London Bridge to Richmond in 1828 was 1s 3d per passenger, for a full boatload of six or eight passengers.

But the steamers were quicker than the boatmen and fairly frequent. Daily, by 1840, there were three in each direction and six by 1843, each carrying about twenty passengers. This pleasant journey was not without drawbacks. Occasionally, if the wind was in the wrong direction, black smoke encompassed the passengers; and it could even be physically dangerous if the boilers burst – as was graphically illustrated in this cartoon.

114. The dangers of travel by river steamer.

115. A steamer leaving Richmond for London in 1832 (engraving by W.B. Cooke from a drawing by J.D. Harding, published in Cooke's *Views of Richmond*).

116. The proposed terminal station at Richmond for the City of London and Richmond Railway, designed by Charles John Blunt, 1836.

117. *The London and South Western Railway station* at Richmond which stood between the Kew Road and Parkshot, in 1936 shortly before its demolition.

118. *Richmond railway stations, c1880*. The terminal station for District, North London, etc. services is on the right; the through tracks of the LSWR are on the left.

The numbers using the steamers were of particular interest to those promoting railway lines in the 1830s and 40s, as indeed were the estimates of coach and omnibus traffic. The first omnibus between Richmond and London was the 'Pilot' in 1830, and at the end of that decade there were five to the Bank and five to St Paul's each day. By 1843 the combined traffic of public coaches and buses on the route was estimated at 1,180,000 passengers a year. This did not include those coaches which plied to places such as Kingston, Hampton Court and Twickenham or the seven carriers' wagons that went to London. It was this traffic, together with that of the river, which the railway promoters aimed to capture.

In 1836 a 'City of London and Richmond Railway' was proposed, from London Bridge to Kew Road, near the new St John's Church. Much of this line would have been carried on a viaduct, and the plan was dropped because of the expense, but it is a pity that the grand classical station proposed for Richmond was never built.

Four years later the London and South Western Railway (LSWR) opened a line from Nine Elms to Southampton, passing through Wimbledon and Kingston (as Surbiton station was first named). In 1844 rival promoters proposed a 'Richmond and West End Junction Railway' which envisaged a link from Richmond to the LSWR line at Falcon Bridge (now Clapham Junction) and then an extension from Nine Elms to a site just south of Waterloo Bridge.

But the LSWR, while supporting this project, insisted that they should themselves build the extension to Waterloo. The 'Richmond Railway' opened in July 1846, Richmond Station being slightly to the south of the present one. The fares to London ranged from 1s first class to 6d third and by the end of 1847 (by which time the line had been absorbed by the LSWR) it was handling 25,000 passengers a month. Another year and an extension was built to Windsor across a railway bridge on the Thames at Richmond. A new station was required for the through line, and this was built between Kew Road and Parkshot.

Richmond's railway network was however far from complete. While the LSWR extended its lines to the west and south-west of Richmond, other railway companies strove to secure a foothold in the Richmond area. The LSWR was however determined to keep control, and agreed only to arrangements that allowed other services into Richmond on its own tracks and on its own terms.

A new line from Willesden to Brentford ('Kew Junction') in 1858 enabled the North London Railway to run trains from Fenchurch Street (and later from Broad Street) into Richmond via Barnes. Under pressure from competitors the LSWR in 1869 built its own line via Kew and Gunnersbury (where a new link was provided for the North London trains) to Hammersmith and Kensington (Addison Road). Eight years later the LSWR permitted the District Railway to link up with its tracks at Hammersmith and so to provide a direct route to Mansion House for Richmond commuters.

For these services yet another Richmond station was built by the LSWR in 1869. Its terminal platforms with their decorated cast-iron roof brackets have survived as part of the new combined station built in 1937.

Richmond, Twickenham, Teddington and Bushey Park, Kingston, Mortlake, Barnes, &c.

Trains proceeding to and from Teddington and Bushey Park, Hampton Wick and Kingston, will be found marked thus, (a) The Journey between Richmond and Kingston occupies 20 minutes

DOWN.	a * 1 2	* 123	a 1 2	a 1	* 1 2	a 1 2	a 1 2	* 1 2	1 2	a 1 2	* 1 2	1 2	a 1 2	a 1 2	a 1 2	* 1 2	* 1 2	* 123	* 123	a 1 2	a 1 2	* 1 2	a 1 2		
From	a.m.	a.m.	a.m.	a.m.	a.m.	a.m.	p.m.	p.m.	p.m.	p.m.	p.m.	p.m.	p.m.	p.m.	p.m.	p.m.	p.m.	p.m	p.m.	p.m.	p.m.	p.m.	p.m.		
WATERLOO	7-35	8- 0	8-40	9-50	10-50	11-20	12-15	12-45	2- 5	2-15	2.40	3.15	4.15	4.50	5 15	5.50	6.35	7-10	7-55	9. 0	10.15	11- 0	12- 0		
Vauxhall	7-41	..	8-46	9.56	10-56	11-26	12-21	12-51	2-11	2-21	2-46	3-21	4.21	..	5.21	..	6.41	7-16	8- 1	9. 6	10 21	11- 6	..	..	..
Clapham Junc.	7-47	..	8 52	..	..	11-32	12-27	..	2-17	2-27	..	3-27	4.27	..	5.27	..	..	7-22	8- 7	9-12	10.27	..	..	..	..
Wandsworth	7-50	..	8-55	10. 5	..	11-35	12-30	..	..	2-30	..	3-30	..	5. 0	5.30	..	..	7-25	..	9.15	10-30	11-15	12-14	..	..
Putney	7-56	..	9 0	10.10	11- 6	11-40	12-35	..	..	2-35	..	3-35	4.34	..	..	6. 5	6.52	7-30	8-12	9.20	10-35	11-20	12-18	..	..
Barnes	8- 1	..	9- 4	10.14	..	11-44	12-39	..	..	2-40	..	3-39	4.38	..	5.37	..	..	7-35	..	9.24	10-39	11-24	12-23	..	..
Mortlake	8- 6	..	9- 8	10.19	..	11.50	12-46	..	..	2-46	..	3-44	4.43	..	5.42	..	6.59	7-40	8.19	9.30	10.45	11-28	12-28	..	..
RICHMOND	8-12	8-20	9-12	10.23	11-16	11.54	12-50	1. 9	2-31	2-52	3- 4	3-48	4.48	5.15	5 46	6.15	7. 5	7-45	8-22	9-35	10.50	11-32	12-32	..	..
Twickenham	8-18	8-27	9-19	10.30	11-22	12. 0	12-57	1.15	2-36	3- 0	3.10	3-55	4.55	5.20	5.52	6.21	7.11	7-52	8.28	9-42	10-55	11-37	12-38	..	.

Trains marked thus * proceed to Windsor. ‡ Come up from Windsor.

UP.	a 1 2	a 1 2 3	1 2 3	‡ 1 2	a 1 2	a 1 2	1 2	a 1 2	‡ 1 2	a 1 2	1 2	‡ 1 2	a 1 2	a 1 2	‡ 1 2 3	a 1 2 3	a 1 2	‡ 1 2	‡ 1 2	a 1 2	‡ 1 2	a 1 2	a 1 2	‡ 1 2	a 1 2	a 1 2
From	a.m.	a.m	a.m	a.m.	a.m	a.m.	a.m.	a.m.	a.m.	a.m.	a.m.	a.m.	p.m	p.m	p.m	p.m	p.m	a. m.	p.m	p.m	a.m.	p.m	p.m	p.m.	p.m	p.m.
Twickenham	7- 0	7-50	..	8-33	8-45	9. 0	9.35	10. 0	10.30	11- 5	11.50	12. 0	1.15	2. 5	3.22	3.40	4. 5	5 24	5.35	6-25	6.51	7-30	8-30	9.10	9-25	10.30
RICHMOND	7- 5	7 55	..	8-40	8-51	9. 5	9.40	10. 6	10.35	11-10	11.55	12. 5	1.20	2.10	3.27	3.45	4 10	5.29	5.40	6-30	6.56	7-35	8-35	9-15	9-30	10.35
Mortlake	7- 9	7-59	..	..	8-55	9.10	..	10.10	..	11-14	..	..	1.24	2.14	..	3.49	4.14	..	5.44	6-34	..	7-39	8-39	..	9-34	10.39
Barnes	7-14	..	8- 15	..	8-58	..	..	..	..	11-21	..	..	1.29	2.21	..	3.54	4.19	..	5 49	6-40	7. 4	7-44	8.44	..	9-39	10.44
Putney	7-18	8- 6	8 -19	..	9- 2	..	..	..	..	11-26	..	..	1.33	2.26	..	3.59	..	5.39	..	6-46	..	7-49	8.48	..	9-44	10.49
Wandsworth	7-23	...	8. 23	..	9- 6	..	..	..	..	11-30	..	..	1.38	2.30	..	4. 3	..	..	..	6-49	..	7-53	8.52	..	9-48	10.53
Clapham Junc.	7-26	..	8 .26	..	9- 9	..	...	..	..	11-33	..	12 17	1.41	2.33	3.43	..	4.29	..	..	...	7.14	7-56	8.55	...	...	...
Vauxhall	7-33	..	8- 33	..	9-16	..	..	..	..	11-40	..	12.23	1 48	2:40	3.50	4.13	4.36	5.50	6. 2	6-59	7.21	8- 3	9. 1	..	9-58	11. 3
WATERLOO	7-40	8-20	8- 40	9- 5	9-23	9 30	10.5	10.30	10 58	11-47	12.19	12.30	1.55	2.48	3.57	4.20	4.43	5.57	6- 8	7- 7	7.28	8 10	9- 8	9-38	10-5	11.10

At the Clapham Junction Passengers can change for Stations on the Main Line to Southampton, Portsmouth, &c.; also for the Crystal Palace, Croydon, and Brighton Lines; and by the West London Extension, for the Great Western, and North Western, and North London Lines. and by the Up Trains to the Victoria Station, Pimlico.

LOOP LINE—Hounslow, Isleworth & Spring Grove, Kew, Barnes, and London.

DOWN.	1 2 3	1 2	1 2	1 2 3	1 2	1 2	1 2	1 2 3	1 2	1 2	1 2	1 2	1 2	1 2	1 2	1 2	1 2	1 2
From	a.m.	a.m.	a.m.	a.m.	a.m.	a.m.	p.m.	p.m.	p.m.	p.m.	p.m.	p.m.	p.m.	p.m.	p.m.	p.m.	p.m.	p.m.
WATERLOO	7-20	8 -30	9. 0	9-35	10-25	11.10	12-15	1.15	2.25	3-45	5- 0	5.35	6.15	6-50	7-30	8.45	9.50	11. 0
Vauxhall	7-26	8 -35	9. 6	9-40	10 31	11 16	12-21	1.21	2.31	3-51	..	..	6.21	..	7-36	8.51	9 56	11. 6
Clapham Jun.	..	..	9.12	9-46	10-37	11-22	12-27	...	..	..	..	..	6.27	..	7-42	..	10. 2	..
Wandsworth..	7-35	8 -44	9.15	9-49	10-40	11.25	12-30	1.30	2.40	4- 0	..	..	6.30	..	7-45	9. 0	10. 5	11.15
Putney	7-39	8 -49	9.20	10-54	10-45	11.30	12-35	1.35	2.45	..	5-14	..	6.35	..	7-50	..	10.10	11.20
Barnes	7-44	8 -53	9.24	10-58	10-49	11.34	12-39	1.40	2.50	4- 6	..	5.50	6.40	..	7-55	9. 6	10.14	11.24
Kew	7-52	—	9.33	10- 2	11- 0	11-45	12-53	1.50	2.59	4-16	5-22	5.59	6.50	7-12	8- 4	9.16	10.23	11.36
Isleworth and Spring Grove	8- 2		9.43	10-11	11- 8	11-56	1- 4	2. 0	3. 9	4-24	5-30	6. 7	7. 0	7-20	8-14	9.24	10.32	11.44
Hounslow ..	8- 7		9.48	10-16	11-15	12- 2	1-10	2. 5	3.14	4-30	5-36	6.13	7. 5	7-26	8-19	9.30	10.37	11 50

UP.	1 2	1 2 3	1 2	1 2	1 2	1 2	1 2	1 2	1 2	1 2 3	1 2	1 2	1 2	1 2	1 2	1 2	1 2	1 2
From	a.m.	a.m.	a.m.	a.m.	a.m	a.m.	a.m.	a.m.	p.m.	p.m.	p.m	p.m.	p.m	p.m	p.m.	p.m	p.m.	p.m.
HOUNSLOW	6.50	7.53	8-35	9. 0	..	9-37	10. 0	11 15	12.15	1. 2	2.10	3-28	4-10	5.45	6-10	7. 0	8-45	10. 0
Isleworth and Spring Grove	6.54	7.57	8-39	9. 4	..	9-41	10. 4	11 19	12.19	1. 6	2.11	3-32	4-14	5.49	6-15	7. 5	8-49	10. 4
Kew	7. 2	8. 5	8-47	9.12	..	9-48	10.11	11 27	12.27	1.14	2.22	3-40	4-22	5.57	6-25	7.15	8-57	10.12
Barnes	7.14	8.13	8-53	9.21	9.22	..	10.19	...	12.36	1.22	2.31	3-47	4-31	6. 4	..	7.23	9- 4	10.21
Putney	7.18	..	8-57	..	9.26	9-57	10.24	11-36	12.41	..	2.36	..	4.36	6. 9	6-37	7.30	9- 8	10.26
Wandsworth ..	7.23	..	..	..	9.30	10- 0	10.29	...	12.45	..	2.40	..	4.41	6.14	..	7.34	9-12	10.30
Clapham Jun.	7.26	...	..	..	..	10- 3	10.32	...	12-48	1-31	2.43	..	4-44	6.18	..	..	9-15	..
Vauxhall ..	7.33	...	..	..	9.39	10-10	10.39	11-48	12.55	1.37	2.50	4- 2	4.51	6.25	6-49	7.43	9 22	10.39
Waterloo......	7.40	8.30	9-10	9.37	9.46	10-17	10.46	11-55	1. 2	1.45	2.57	4- 8	4.58	6-32	6-55	7.50	9.30	10-45

NORTH LONDON RAILWAY.

Richmond, Kingston, Bushey Park, Teddington, Twickenham, and London.

All Trains by this Line go on to Kingston.

DOWN TRAINS.

Fenchurch St.	8 0	10. 0	12. 0	2. 0	4.15	5.15	6. 0	7.45	8. 0
Kew	9.15	11.15	1.15	3.15	5.10	6.10	7.15	9. 0	9.15
Mortlake	9.29	11.29	1 29	3.29	5.24	6.27	7.34	9.14	9.37
Richmond ..	9.34	11.34	1.34	3 34	5.29	6.32	7.39	9.19	9.42
Twickenham	940	11.40	1.40	3.40	5.35	6.38	7.45	9.25	9.48

UP TRAINS.

Twickenham	7.40	8 28	10 5	12. 5	1.55	3.55	6. 5	7. 0	8. 5
Richmond ..	7.45	8 .33	10.10	12 10	2. 0	4. 0	6.10	7. 5	8 10
Mortlake	7.50	8 37	10.15	12.15	2. 5	4. 5	6.15	7.10	8.15
Kew	8 5	9 5	10.30	12.30	2.30	4.30	6.30	7.30	8.30
Fenchurch St.	8.55	9 55	11.40	1 40	3.40	5 40	7.40	8.40	9.40

By this Line passengers are taken to and from Acton, Finchley Road, Hampstead, Kentish Town, Camden Road, &c.

119. Timetables of trains servicing the Richmond area in 1863 (at this time the North London trains ran through to Kingston on the LSWR tracks).

120. Electric trams from Kew Bridge to Shepherd's Bush, introduced in 1901, were the first in London.

BUSES AND TRAMS IN RICHMOND

The river steamers did not survive the competition, at least as a commuter service, but the horse buses did. And, from 1883 until 1912 horse trams operated between Kew Bridge and the Orange Tree pub in Richmond. In 1901 a new electric tramway, the first in London, was opened from the far end of Kew Bridge to Shepherd's Bush. Approval for their service was held up for some time because of the fear that the electric trams would interfere with the magnetic instruments at Kew Observatory. It took several tests, the last one involving the running of thirty trams, before the Kew authorities professed themselves satisfied.

The big change came in the early twentieth century, when motor buses began to rival the railways – by 1914 Richmond's streets were crowded with them and they could barely scrape past each other on the narrow Richmond Bridge.

121. *A horse bus*, plying between Richmond and Kingston, outside the Orange Tree public house in Kew Road.

Richmond's Inns and Taverns

Catering for visitors has been a Richmond industry since the sixteenth century. The main inns of Queen Elizabeth's time must have been the Red Lyon and the Bell (in what is now George Street), which were used to house the Duke of Anjou's retinue when he came, in vain, to claim the Queen's hand in 1581. Others, such as the Golden Hind (later Feathers) in King Street, the Rose and Crown (at the corner of Duke Street), the Lily Pot (at the corner of Brewer's Lane), flourished in the seventeenth century, but the Red Lyon maintained its supremacy until it closed in the 1720s. (The name was revived in the 1750s for a smaller tavern in what is now Red Lion Street.)

There were smaller alehouses around the Green and in King and George Streets. The Justices for Surrey reported to the Privy Council in 1634 that 'they had already licensed only twenty-five alehouses in the fifteen parishes of the Kingston and Elmbridge hundreds', yet 'within Richmond, by reason of the Prince's Court often residing there and being a place of much resort and recreation for divers gentlemen and citizens, of the twenty-five they have licensed ten there'.

122. *The old Red Lyon Inn*, stretching round the corner of George Street and Red Lion Street, can be seen in the centre of this detail from *The Prospect of Richmond*, 1726. The Feathers Inn, at the end of King Street, is partly visible behind the large tree to the right of the Red Lyon.

123. Thomas R. Way's drawing of the Red Lion tavern in 1900.

126. The yard at the back of the Greyhound *c*1800 (watercolour by Jean Claude Nattes, now on loan to the Museum of Richmond from the Ionides Collection at Orleans House).

GREYHOUND HOTEL.
Established 1685.
FOR FAMILIES & GENTLEMEN.
Excellent Cuisine. :: Moderate Tariff.
✥ STABLING AND GARAGE. ✥
— Telephone : 324 P.O. RICHMOND. —

124. An early twentieth-century advertisement for the Greyhound Hotel.

125. *The Talbot Hotel* (from an engraved letterhead).

Two major new inns were established in Richmond early in the eighteenth century. The name of the old White Horse tavern on the Green was transferred to a new house in the main street near the entrance to Church Court; this was renamed (and probably rebuilt) as the Greyhound about 1725 and survived as inn and hotel until 1923. It had become one of the important meeting places of the town, its Assembly Room used as a Masonic Hall, the venue of the Parish Trustees, and the place where the Richmond Cricket Club was founded in 1862 and the Richmond Golf Club in 1891. The building was restored as offices in 1983–84.

The Dog Inn, opposite the top of Ferry Hill, can be traced back to 1702, but may well have been founded earlier. *The Prospect of Richmond* (see p. 32) shows that it already had extensive buildings in 1726. It became the Talbot in the 1730s or 40s and survived as a hotel into the twentieth century; but part of it was converted into the Talbot Cinema in 1914, and the remainder replaced by the Richmond (now Odeon) Cinema in 1930.

127. *The Black Horse Inn*, c1830 (lithograph by Janson and Danvers).

128. *The Roebuck*, c1720 (detail from the Laurence Knyff painting on p25).

129. The top end of King Street in 1900, showing on the left the former Feathers Inn, by then converted into offices, and on the right the Old Ship tavern.

Only a few of the many historic Richmond pubs can be shown here. Two of the oldest, still operating under their original names, on their original sites (though rebuilt), are the Black Horse, established at Marshgate on the road to East Sheen about 1720, and the Roebuck on the Terrace of Richmond Hill, which dates from about the same time.

King Street was a favourite location for taverns. At the corner of Water Lane stood the Golden Hind (probably named for Drake's ship, but the owner of the land on which it was built in the reign of Elizabeth I was John Hynde). This became the Feathers, possibly an allusion to the badge of the Prince of Wales, then occupying Richmond Palace. It was partly rebuilt in the eighteenth century, converted into offices in the 1850s, and was demolished for road widening in 1907. Next door stood the Six Bells, first mentioned in 1682: this changed its name to the Ship in 1724, and, as the Old Ship, has flourished from 1766 to the present day. (It once had a rival called the New Ship at 12–13 King Street.)

The Castle in George Street had two Jacobean gables, one of which survives at what is now No. 37. About 1760 its proprietor, John Halford, moved the name and licence to a mansion in Hill Street and the Castle Inn then developed into Richmond's leading hotel in the town centre. Assembly Rooms were built on the northern side of its gardens, which stretched to the boathouses on the riverside. Balls, concerts and famous parties were given here, including a grand fête hosted by the Austrian ambassador to celebrate Queen Victoria's coronation, and a special entertainment for the Commissioners of the Great Exhibition in 1851. By then it had been taken over by Joseph Ellis, owner of the Star and Garter, who rebuilt the Assembly Rooms.

130. *The Castle Hotel* fronting on Hill Street, in 1866 (engraving by Rook & Co.).

131. *The Austrian Ambassador's fête at the Castle Hotel* in honour of Queen Victoria's coronation. The assembly rooms are the range on the left; in the background is the rear of the main hotel building. (Engraving by H. Adlard from a drawing by T. Allom *c*1838.)

The Castle's fortunes waned in the 1870s and it was closed as a hotel in 1876, though the Assembly Rooms and dining room remained open. In 1888 the hotel building was bought by Sir John Whittaker Ellis and presented to the town as a site for the new municipal offices.

The famous Star and Garter Hotel began as a smallish tavern, built in 1738 on Petersham Common by John Christopher (already a successful Richmond publican). It flourished and about 1770 a new building was added, and the modest tavern became an inn. A ballroom and dining room were built in 1803, work which bankrupted the owner, but after five years it was reopened by Christopher Crean, former chef to the Duke of York. In 1815 it was described as 'a very costly house', with the drawback that 'the company who frequent it' were 'rather select than numerous'. That was changed after Joseph Ellis bought it from Crean's widow in 1822. He enlarged the residential accommodation, building a new wing at the back, and terraced the garden overlooking the river. He attracted company that was numerous as well as select and made so much money he was able to buy the Castle Hotel as well.

After Ellis's death the hotel was managed for a few years by one of his sons, who then sold it to a company in 1864. Their first act was to commission a large new block to replace the oldest buildings,

132. *Joseph Ellis*, proprietor of the Star and Garter (and later of the Castle also).

designed by E.M. Barry in 'French chateau' style. He also built a banqueting hall at the northern end of the late-eighteenth and early-nineteenth-century buildings. It was these latter buildings which were destroyed in the great fire in February 1870, but the 1864 additions were largely undamaged. The gap left by the fire was not replaced by residential accommodation, but by a pavilion containing an enormous dining room. Designed by C.J. Phipps in what was described as 'Italian romanesque' style, it could seat 250 diners in the main hall and many more in the thirteen private rooms leading off the balcony. This was now the Star and Garter's main business; though it still had many residential guests – some of them crowned heads – the money lay in catering to London society out on a drive to Richmond for the day or evening. Perhaps the advent of the motor car, which gave those same people a greater range for their outings, was responsible for its demise. By 1907 it was up for sale and although it was said to have cost over £130,000 to build the best offer was only £20,000. It closed down and was used as a hospital during the first World War. The subsequent history will be found on p. 87.

133. (Top) The original Star and Garter tavern is on the right of this anonymous mid-eighteenth-century drawing.

134. (Middle) *A Day's Pleasure* was the title of this engraving of a private party at the Star and Garter, from a painting by E. Prentis, 1842.

135. (Bottom) Barry's building at the Star and Garter, built in 1865, seen from inside the gates of Richmond Park.

136. *The Richmond Hill Hotel* (now the Petersham) in 1868.

The Richmond Hill Hotel Company purchased Nightingale Lodge in 1863 – this stood on the slope of the Hill below The Wick. On its site was built in 1865 another large hotel, designed by John Giles, among whose other work was the Langham Hotel in Portland Place (happily now renovated). Built in a style betraying French chateau and romanesque influences, it fitted well into the scene below Barry's Star and Garter. Its most notable feature was the great unsupported stone staircase, with ceiling murals painted by a Signor Galli.

The Richmond Hill Hotel was renamed The Mansion in the 1870s and, in 1924, the New Star and Garter. From 1978 it has been The Petersham and has been extensively restored and brought up to 'four-star' standard.

Thackeray's favourite Richmond hotel was the Rose Cottage in Friars Stile Road, which had been, since the 1820s, a tea garden run by Marie Gibbins. It developed into a hotel in 1840s, still under Mrs Gibbins. Thackeray described it in 1844 as 'one of the comfortablest, quietest, cheapest, neatest little inns in England, and a thousand times preferable, in my opinion, to the Star and Garter…I quitted [it] with deep regret, believing that I should see nothing so pleasant as its gardens and its veal cutlets, and its dear little bowling green, elsewhere.' In the 1870s Mrs Gibbins changed its title to the Marlborough, and under that name it still survives as a public house, with an extensive garden.

A rival to the Castle and the Talbot, from 1834 to the 1850s, was the Royal Hotel, converted from the mansion built in the 1820s for Joshua Smith (Lord Mayor of London 1810–11) on the site of the most southerly of the three Heron Court houses. In 1838 a developer, L.W. Lloyd, acquired the hotel and adjoining land by Bridge and Hill Streets, and built Royal Terrace, which stretched from the entrance to Heron Court, round the corner into Bridge Street. It included a new arcaded entrance to the hotel from Hill Street, a hotel tap, kitchens and stabling as well as ten shops. However, Lloyd bankrupted himself doing this and the hotel never really recovered. By the mid-1850s the Royal was split into three houses, one being merged into the new Tower House. The facade of the old mansion was, however, preserved in the recent development.

Where there are so many taverns and inns then there are breweries. The principal Richmond brewery of the eighteenth and early nineteenth centuries was founded in the 1720s by the Collins family at the bottom of Water Lane – to the indignation of neighbours who united to protest against the 'smoak, filth and stench' it emitted, but to no avail. The brewery continued on the site, expanded up Water Lane and was closed only in the 1870s when the Richmond Vestry bought it for their new water works headquarters.

Opposite it, across the little town wharf, the White Cross tavern was built in the 1760s. Rebuilt in the 1830s and subsequently enlarged by an extra storey, it still stands. It was one of several Richmond public houses that enjoyed a brief existence as small hotels after cycling became a craze in the late nineteenth century.

137. *The Marlborough Hotel*, formerly Rose Cottage, in Friar's Stile Road.

138. *The Royal Hotel* as shown in an advertisement of 1842.

139. *The White Cross tavern and Collins' brewery* in the 1840s.

A Place for Learning

PLENTIFUL SCHOOLS

The first school in Richmond of which there is any record at all was that for Chapel Royal choristers, mentioned in a document of 1581: this may have been in the former Friary. In the mid-seventeenth century a number of schoolmasters can be found in the pew-lists, the parish registers and other records, and one schoolroom is identifiable in the manor records of 1665 in the garden behind No. 1 The Green. These were all private schools; an offer to found a free charity school was made in 1658, but lapsed with the would-be founder's death three years later.

It was in 1713 that a free charity school, linked to the parish church, was eventually founded from a public subscription, to which Queen Anne and most of the town's leading inhabitants (including Elihu Yale) subscribed. The old Lily Pot inn at the north corner of George Street and Brewer's Lane was purchased as a site and Dr Nicholas Brady, Minister of Richmond, was its first headmaster.

Pupils dressed in blue gowns, and wore small round, numbered, metal badges. St Mary's parochial school remained here until 1854 when it went to new buildings at the top of the newly-developed Eton Street. By then it was known as a 'National School', as were all Anglican parish schools assisted by the National Society, set up for that purpose in 1811. Other early National schools were St John's in Clarence Street, the Queen's School at Kew and a small establishment at Ham.

140. A badge worn by a pupil at the free parochial school, founded in 1713. (Museum of Richmond).

141. *The National Schools* at the junction of Paradise Road and Eton Street (now the site of Eton House).

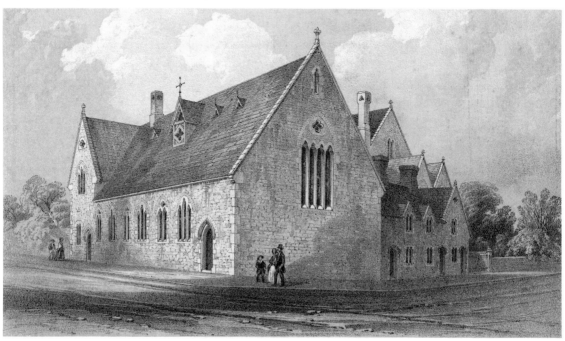

142. *The British Schools*, built in The Vineyard in 1867

143. *The Russell British School* at Petersham.

Not everyone supported the concept of exclusively Anglican education for the poor, and the British and Foreign School Society helped to set up non-denominational schools, 'British Schools'. The first of these in the area was at Petersham, built at the expense of Lord John Russell, who then lived at Pembroke Lodge in Richmond Park. The original building in 'Petersham Park' was the all-brick one shown in the photograph here – the half-timbered extension was added later. It was destroyed by bombs in November 1943 and rebuilt on a new site near the gates of Ham House.

A group of Richmond people, mainly non-conformists, founded the Richmond British School in 1867 in the Vineyard. The Vineyard School was moved to Friars Stile Road in the 1980s, but its original buildings have survived, converted into housing.

But private schools were the most numerous in Richmond. There was hardly a large house in the entire town that was not a school at some time in its history. John Evans, in his guide *Richmond and its Vicinity*, published in 1824, listed a score of them in Richmond, two in Petersham and one in Ham, as well as fifteen private tutors.

Perhaps the best known of these was Richmond Academy, run from 1764 by a succession of clergymen of the Delafosse family in a mansion at the corner of Little Green and Duke Street. Among its pupils was Richard Burton, the famous Arabist, who left an amusing account of how he and his brothers, then living in Maids of Honour Row, would take to school with them the remains of the previous night's dinner, including the wine.

After the retirement of the third Delafosse in 1838, the house became for a while a Royal Navy school for girls, called Hope House. Then in 1856 it was purchased to become a Cavalry College, but was almost at once destroyed by fire. A splendid new building for the College was built in 1857, but the venture was unsuccessful and closed in 1860, and for the next half century various kinds of school resided here. Onslow Hall, the name it still retains, was a military preparatory college for Sandhurst and Woolwich from 1897 to 1912.

144. *Richmond Academy* (from Beresford Chancellor's *History and Antiquities of Richmond, etc.*, 1894).

145. The architect's design for the Cavalry College in 1857. The wings were never built. (Engraving from the *Illustrated London News*.)

The first public secondary school in Richmond was the County Secondary School for Boys, built in 1896 in the Kew Road. This became a Technical Institute in 1939, and after the war served as an Institute of Further Education and an Adult College, before being converted into housing. In Parkshot, in 1908–09, the first girls' County School was built, although this was a descendant of a private school founded in 1861. It in turn became the Adult College in 1974.

One of the first attempts at adult education was the Mechanics' Institute, erected in 1843 on the site of the old town pond. Perhaps more appropriately the building was converted to the public baths from 1855 to 1867, and since then, with an upper floor added, it has been Assembly Rooms, shops, auction room, furniture store, cinema and offices. The dome added in 1908 gave it its present name of Dome Buildings.

BOOKS FOR THE PEOPLE

Richmond was one of the first local authorities in the London area to establish a free public library, built on a vacant site by Little Green in 1881. It is ironic to note that the Vestry recommended its Library Committee to 'consider utilizing the unoccupied ground at the rear of the Free Library for the erection of a Museum or of an Athenaeum and School of Art'. A room had indeed been set aside for a museum in the Mechanics' Institute forty years earlier; but on neither occasion was the idea followed up. Richmond had to wait more than a hundred years before a museum was finally established.

146. *The County Secondary School for Boys* in Kew Road, Richmond – architect's design. The hall on the right was not built in 1896; and a larger hall to a different design was added later.

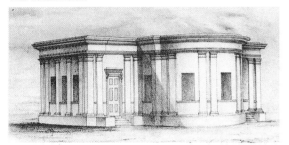

147. The original building of the *Mechanics' Institute*, 1843.

148. The interior of the *Richmond Public Library* in 1884.

149. *The Richmond Free Public Library*, design by F.S. Brunton, 1881 (from *The Builder*).

Places of Care

THE ROYAL HOSPITAL

The origin of the Royal Hospital lay in a £40 balance left over from the subscription for a dinner on Richmond Green for the schoolchildren and the poor to celebrate the marriage of the Prince of Wales in 1863! A committee was set up to consider using this to help found a small hospital and after a while an offer was made to let to them a mansion called Rosedale, former home of the Earl and Countess of Shaftesbury (and once of James Thomson, the poet), for £100 per year. Or it might be bought for £2,100. An appeal was launched, the money raised, and in February 1868 the hospital was opened by the Earl and Countess Russell.

It soon acquired royal patronage. Just as a new ward, to be named after Princess May of Teck (the future Queen Mary) who had been active in fund-raising, was about to be completed it was announced that Queen Victoria herself had agreed to become patron and henceforth the hospital was 'The Royal Hospital'. It expanded until the 1960s; but in the next decade a number of its facilities were closed until in 1982 demolition was threatened. The hospital was saved, but for out-patient treatment only.

150. *'Rosedale' in Kew Foot Road, in about 1820.*

151. *The Royal Hospital* in 1898 (from Somers Gascoyne's *Recollections of Richmond*).

152. *The Workhouse Infirmary*, 1902.

153. A photograph taken at the Infirmary when it was partly used as a military hospital during the Great War.

THE WORKHOUSE INFIRMARY

The Richmond Workhouse had had, from 1787, a sick ward, but in 1902 the Guardians of the Richmond Union commissioned an Infirmary to be built on the workhouse garden. It was to consist of two main blocks, for male and female patients, with three separate pavilions – two of which contained maternity and lunatic wards. A special feature of the two main blocks were wards for consumptives in the penthouse pavilions, which could be opened to the air.

This building, designed by E.J. Partridge, cost £40,000 and was opened on 6 December 1902. It provided accommodation for 174 patients. During the first World War part of it was used as a military hospital and in 1948, when workhouses were abolished, it became the Grove Road Hospital, specialising in the care of the aged. It was finally closed in June 1974; two of the original blocks remain, converted into housing.

1. View of the Home from the Common.—2. Scrubbing the Dormitories.—3. In the Laundry.—4. In the Playground.

A VISIT TO THE NATIONAL ORPHAN HOME, HAM COMMON, SURREY

154. *The National Orphan Home* at Ham (from *The Graphic*, 11 July 1874).

THE ORPHANS

The site of South Lodge in Ham was that on which in 1838 a Pestalozzi school was founded. It grew into a commune called 'Concordium', which aimed for a self-supporting life of austerity, vegetarianism and celibacy, turning away from industrialism and materialism. In this it was inspired by the ideas of Robert Owen and James Pierrepont Greaves. However, by 1848, the community was disbanded.

John Minter Morgan of Ham bought the site to provide a home for girls orphaned in the cholera epidemic of 1848–49, but its scope was subsequently extended to include those orphaned by the Crimean War. In the 1860s, in a new building, it became the National Orphan Home for Girls. It has now been converted into flats, while Morgan's own house, West Heath, after a period of use as a private girls' school, became in 1948 the Hospital of the Cassel Foundation, specialising in psychiatric disorders.

LOOKING AFTER THE DISABLED

During the first World War the empty Star and Garter Hotel was bought in 1915 by public subscription (on the initiative of the Auctioneers and Estate Agents' Institute) and presented to Queen Mary to found a home for disabled servicemen. The British Red Cross managed the project; the pavilion and banqueting hall were quickly converted into wards, and the home was opened in January 1916. But it was not a building which could economically meet the needs of peacetime, and it was decided to rebuild entirely rather than convert. The patients and staff were moved temporarily to Sandgate. The new building, designed free of charge by Sir Edwin Cooper, was formally opened by George V and Queen Mary in July 1924 under the name of the Royal Star and Garter Home for Disabled Sailors, Soldiers and Airmen.

155. King George V and Queen Mary talking to patients at the opening of the Star and Garter Home in 1924.

156. Sir Edwin Cooper's sketch of the new Star and Garter Home.

Suburban Growth

Richmond grew at a steady pace until the mid-nineteenth century. A population of 4628 in 1801 had doubled to 9255 fifty years later. Most of this increase was in the old built-up area. New houses were, for instance, built in streets off the southern end of the Kew Road, near the new St John's Church, and in courts and alleys off Red Lion Street and Paradise Road.

However, 'New Richmond' was developed in the 1820s on new ground. It was on the south side of the Lower Mortlake Road, about midway between the Kew Road and Manor Road corners, and here several rows of small villas and cottages were built for the working-class population. In the 1840s came the first development in the fields higher up the Hill. Park Road was made to link Friars Stile Road and Queens Road, Park Villas were built on the west side of Queens Road, and Rothesay Villas in Friars Stile Road.

Then came the railway. The Richmond Upper Field (from the Lower Mortlake Road to the Hill top) disappeared beneath streets of large and medium-sized villas for middle class Londoners anxious to commute from the country instead. New estates were developed in the grounds of large houses – and the new roads were named after the houses: Halford Road, the Hermitage, Ellerker Gardens, Mount Ararat Road. By the end of the nineteenth century no open building land was left in the Upper Field apart from the grounds of a few remaining mansions. And when Kew Gardens station opened in 1886 the area along the Kew Road was rapidly built up.

158. *Cottages in Sheendale Road*, New Richmond.

159. *Nos. 20–34 Friar's Stile Road*.

157. *Hermitage Villas*, built in the grounds of The Hermitage.

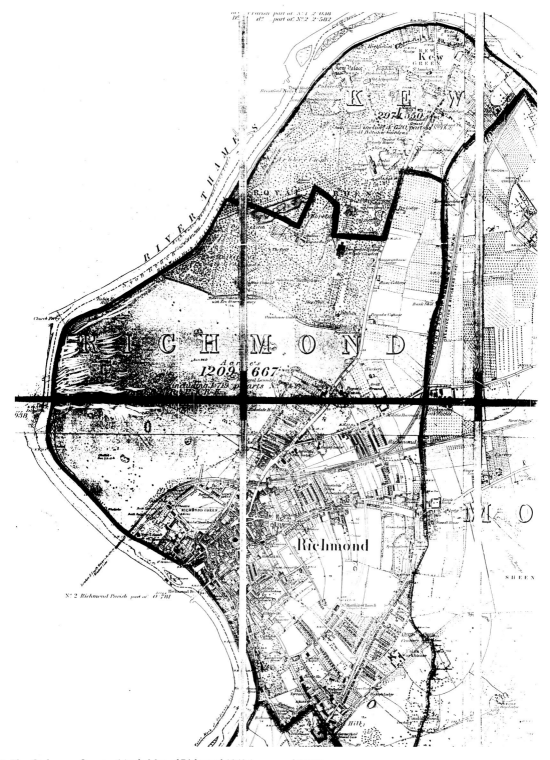

160. The Ordnance Survey 6-inch *Map of Richmond* 1869 (surveyed 1863).

One area ripe for development was land given by George III to the Vestry on Pesthouse Common. Part of it was reserved until 1834 for the workhouse farm, and part was eventually to be used for a new burial ground, but there was from the outset a lot of extra land let as pasture.

In the 1840s, after the workhouse had been transferred to the new Union (see p. 48) and the farm given up, the Vestry realised that revenue could be had from the vacant land. Permission to use the land for building had to be sought from the Court of Chancery; this was given in 1845 and the first building leases for Pesthouse Common were granted in 1850. The hopes of rapid development were dashed by the outbreak of the Crimean War. One would-be developer, Somers Gascoyne, appealing for a reduction in his ground rent, spoke of 'the great depression in the building trade'. However, by 1863 there was a continuous line of villas down Queen's Road from the Lass of Richmond Hill pub to the northern corner of Grove Road, and the new Cambrian, Park Hill, Pyrland and Greville Roads had been built, mostly with large detached or semi-detached houses.

Meanwhile, in the town centre, many of the old cottages had become unwholesome slums. A Vestry report in 1868 drew attention to the unsatisfactory and insanitary conditions in the area between the Kew Road and Kew Foot Road (Michel's Buildings, Obligation Row, Perseverance Place, Night and Morning Row – which was pulled down), in Water Lane and Whitecross Row and, by then, in 'New Richmond' as well.

161. *'Bug Island'* – shortly before demolition in 1889.

162. Some of the large mansions on the Parish Lands estate on Queen's Road can be seen in the centre of this view from the tower of St Matthias' church. The workhouse is in the background.

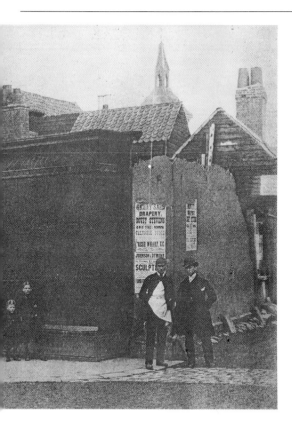

The group of cottages which had grown up from the late sixteenth century between the junction of the Kew and Marshgate (Sheen) Roads had the nickname 'Bug Island', which neatly summed up its sanitary state (it was officially called Middle Row). In 1889–90 almost all of it was swept away, although its last remaining eighteenth-century building lasted exactly another century.

When the new Magistrates' Court was built on the site of the Vestry Hall in 1896 Paradise Road was widened, and this acted as a spur for the launching of a project by Somers Gascoyne (by then an Alderman) to drive a new highway from there to the end of the bridge, at the same time demolishing what he described as 'a great block of dilapidated and insanitary hovels in Red Lion Street'. Gascoyne's highway project was never carried out (though it was still being talked of in the 1960s), but in 1909–12 the Red Lion Street improvement scheme was implemented, with the road widened and straightened. Artichoke Alley and Ormond Passage were razed and Lewis and Wakefield Roads and Victoria Place were built.

163. One of the last of the 19th-century villas on the Queen's Road estate, before demolition in 1976.

164. *Artichoke Alley* (from Somers Gascoyne's *Recollections of Richmond*, c1899).

An early scheme to provide better and affordable housing for the working classes was a private philanthropic project. The militia headquarters in the Lower Mortlake Road, built in castellated style in 1856 and called Castle Gate, was given up in 1875, and in the 1880s it was acquired by Thomas Cave MP (who lived in Queensberry House) for conversion into thirty-seven separate dwellings. Castlegate Dwellings, as they were called, were demolished in 1909. The need had by then been met by the Council.

165. *'Castlegate'* in the early twentieth century.

THE RICHMOND EXPERIMENT

In the year Richmond became a borough, 1890, the Housing of the Working Classes Act was passed. This gave local councils not only the power to close and demolish insanitary premises but, for the first time, the facility to acquire land and build houses for lease at 'fair rents' to the working class. Thanks primarily to the initiative of William Thompson, councillor and future mayor of Richmond, the borough was one of the first in the country, and the very first in the London area, to take advantage of the Act.'The Richmond Experiment' as it became known, consisted of sixty single cottages and six dwellings of upper and lower flats, in and off Manor Road on land which had once been part of George III's farm, in that area of Mortlake transferred to Richmond in 1892.

The project, financed by loans, was self-supporting and was acclaimed a great success. As soon as the first houses were occupied in 1896, the building of another seventy along the new Manor Grove was agreed. Quite a lot of other Council housing followed before World War I.

166. *The 'Richmond Experiment'*: some of the first council houses in Manor Grove (from Somers Gascoyne's *Recollections of Richmond, c*1899).

167. *The Church of St John the Divine*, Kew Road, Richmond (engraving by H. Kernot from a drawing by T. Allom, c1840).

168. *St Matthias's Church* (engraving by Rook & Co., c1862).

THE NEW CHURCHES

Despite new aisles and galleries in the parish church of Richmond, accommodation remained a problem as the population expanded rapidly in the early nineteenth century. In the late 1820s it was decided to build a new church. Lewis Vulliamy was engaged as architect to build St John the Divine on the Kew Road at what was then almost the northern end of the town; it was consecrated in 1836 – and made into a new parish two years later.

But, in an age of church-going, this met the demand for a few years only. By the mid–1850s another church was needed for the population on the hill. At the end of Friars Stile Road, on land given by Charles Jasper Selwyn (a future Lord Justice of Appeal), the church of St Matthias, designed by Sir George Gilbert Scott in Gothic style, with a high tower and spire still a landmark today, was opened in 1858.

169. The Congregational and Roman Catholic Churches in The Vineyard in 1832. St Elizabeth's Church was greatly enlarged and given a new tower in 1903.

170. *Rehoboth Strict Baptist Chapel*, Parkshot

171. The *Baptist Church* in Duke Street, built in 1881 and replaced by a new church building in 1961–62.

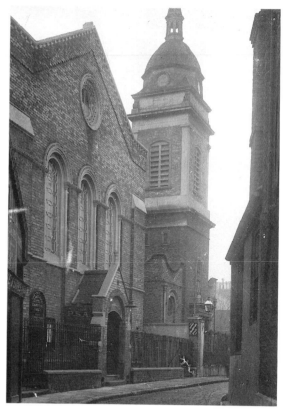

172. The Congregational and Roman Catholic Churches in The Vineyard, *c*1910.

Other Anglican churches followed: Holy Trinity in Sheen Park in 1870, St Luke's in the Avenue, Kew, in 1888, Christ Church in the Kew Road in 1893.

As already noted, the old playhouse on the Hill became a dissenters' meeting hall. A Roman Catholic chapel had been established in the Vineyard, and in 1797 a small independent Calvinist chapel was built in Ormond Passage. Then, in 1824, Miss Elizabeth Doughty (of Doughty House on the Terrace) provided land in the Vineyard and built at her own expense a proper Roman Catholic church, St Elizabeth's. Seven years later a Congregational church was erected next door.

A Strict Baptist Chapel, Rehoboth, was established in Parkshot in 1829. Another Baptist congregation met briefly in the meeting room of the public baths (the old Mechanics' Institute) in 1862, but was dispersed after a few months. Then in 1867 the congregation was reformed, meeting in the lecture hall in Hill Street. A couple of years later the Baptists purchased land in Park Lane, off Parkshot, and erected there an 'iron church' purchased in – and moved from – Teddington. It was succeeded in 1881 by a much larger building in Duke Street, designed on an octagonal plan, with a pyramidal dome and lantern and two towers, one with a spire.

173. *The Wesleyan Institute, c1840* (engraving by H. Adlard from a drawing by T. Allom).

Wesleyans met in various rented rooms from 1810 onwards. Later on, in 1843, a large Wesleyan theological college was built on Richmond Hill, designed in gothic style by Andrew Trimmer; and seven years later a public chapel was added at the Friars Stile Road end of the grounds. This chapel was destroyed by bombs in 1940, but by then another Wesleyan chapel had been built in the Kew Road. The Wesleyan college was closed in 1972; but is now, as 'Richmond College', an American international campus.

The small Wesleyan chapel in Petersham which existed from 1866 to 1891 is notable as having been sketched by Vincent Van Gogh, who preached there (as he also did in the Kew Road chapel) during his visit to England in 1876.

174. *The Wesleyan Chapel in Petersham*, sketch by Vincent van Gogh, 1876.

175. *St Andrew's Church, Ham*, as originally built in 1831.

There was no church at Ham until 1831, when the Countess of Dysart gave land on Ham Common for the building of St Andrew's, to the designs of Edward Lapidge.

The largest church in the Richmond area has never been consecrated. In 1894 Mrs Lionel Warde of Petersham House bought Bute House and its extensive grounds on the south side of the Petersham Road. She demolished the house, and – believing that Petersham would soon be developed as intensively as Richmond – she set out to build a new church, at the southern end of the estate, to serve as a centre for the new population and as a memorial to her parents. All Saints' Church, designed by John Kelly as a romanesque basilica, with a high campanile, was finished in 1908; but the new population never materialised and the church was not consecrated. It was used as a radar training centre for Anti-Aircraft Command during World War II.

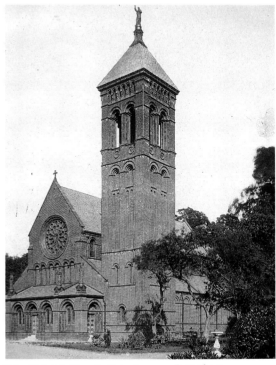

176. *All Saints Church*, Bute Avenue, Petersham.

THE SHOPS

Richmond was never a market town, for Kingston's market was granted by charter a monopoly within a seven-mile radius. It has however developed as a local shopping centre.

The first shops that can be identified as such in the Richmond manor records were located on, or just off, the Green in the reigns of Elizabeth I and James I. In 1586 a shop is mentioned on the site of No. 25 The Green; in 1612 one at No. 1 The Green; and in 1617 four shops (which may have been in existence in 1586) stood at the end of Brewer's Lane (on the sites of Nos 12–18).

In the seventeenth and eighteenth century shops developed along Cross Street (later Furbelow Street and now King Street), in some of the cottages facing the west side of London or Great Street (now George Street) and at the foot of Hill Street. These three streets remained Richmond's whole shopping area until the developments of the mid-nineteenth century.

An analysis of the trades mentioned in the parish registers in the first decade of the eighteenth century shows that, apart from many persons connected with building , and such trades as farrier and blacksmith, the shops at that time would have included apothecaries, barbers, tailors, glovers, hatters, drapers, many shoemakers, grocers and chandlers, and food shops such as butchers, poulterers, fishmongers, bakers and a pastrycook.

The most famous shop of eighteenth and nineteenth century Richmond was that at No. 3 Hill Street where the cheese-flavoured tartlets called 'Maids of Honour' were made, according to a secret recipe, and sold; for over two hundred years this was run by three families of pastrycooks: Bullen, Burdekin and Billet.

177. *The Maids of Honour shop* in the early nineteenth century.

178. *Lotz, confectioners*, in Hill Street, *c*1890.

179. *Hill Street* in 1897

180. *William Robertson's shop* at Nos 46–47 George Street in 1837.

181. *George Street, c*1900.

New local shopping areas were opened up for the new communities on the Hill, in New Richmond and round Kew Gardens Station. In central Richmond shops began to spread up the lower reaches of the Hill and along the Petersham Road, quite often in the front gardens of the old houses, as extensions to the houses. At the other end of the town shops began to appear in the Kew Road, around the railway station and the new St John's Church. On the west side of Kew Road, between Duke Street and the railway bridge, W.H. Rydon built in 1876–77 an imposing new terrace of shops called 'The Quadrant', replacing a few old buildings and workshops.

Richmond's first bank, the London and County, was established in 1852 in Hill Street, taking over part of the offices of Ellis's wine business. The vine, planted against the building in 1840, survived wartime bombing and the consequent complete rebuilding and still grows by the wall of what is now the National Westminster Bank.

183. *The Quadrant*, Kew Road.

184. Shops developed up Hill Rise about a hundred years ago.

182. The building at 9 Hill Street which housed Ellis's wine business, with a meeting hall above – and in which Richmond's first bank was established in 1852.

185. *The Petersham village shop.*

186. *Gosling's store* at Nos 78–80 George Street in 1892.

As was the trend in other towns, some of Richmond's original drapers' shops grew into department stores. Gosling's drapery, opened in 1795 at No. 80 George Street, expanded into adjacent buildings and even into the Queens Head pub at the corner of King Street. After a bad fire in the 1960s Gosling's finally closed down in 1968 and the premises were rebuilt as the new Dickens and Jones store in 1970 (see p. 135).

Frederick and Arthur Wright opened a drapers' business in George Street in 1877. Over the years this expanded into buildings on both sides of the street, but was finally consolidated in the large store at Nos 29–33. This was later taken over by Owen Owen, who closed down in 1990.

A large business which had its first roots in Richmond was the Perring furniture chain. In 1895 John Perring took over a group of five little shops in Paved Court and named them 'Noah's Ark Stores'. Within a few years he acquired extra premises in the Kew Road, and it is said that he personally strung wires over the intervening roofs to link his stores and warehouses by telephone. Soon Perring stores were established in many other towns. The original Noah's Ark Stores were taken over by Gosling's in 1960.

187. *Wright Brothers'* two stores in George Street in the early twentieth century.

Richmond Becomes a Borough

The new responsibilities gradually heaped on the old Parish Vestry were stretching its resources. Like other villages in the London area which had become sizable and thriving towns, Richmond needed to be reformed as a borough with the appropriate statutory powers, and this was the view expressed by a meeting of ratepayers in 1877. In the simple matter of accommodation action was needed, for the Vestry Hall in Paradise Road was too small, and for some years the Vestry toyed with the idea of buying the Castle Hotel after it was closed in 1876 for use as a new headquarters, but they could not afford the price asked.

188. *'The Charter of Incorporation is brought to Richmond'* on 23 July 1890 (from the *Richmond and Twickenham Times*).

189. Notice of the public enquiry on the petition for incorporation, 1888.

PARISH OF RICHMOND.

PROPOSED

INCORPORATION.

NOTICE IS HEREBY GIVEN, that the Honourable T. H. W. PELHAM, Barrister-at-law, the Commissioner appointed by the Lords of Her Majesty's Privy Council, will open an Inquiry at the VESTRY HALL, Paradise Road, Richmond, Surrey, on TUESDAY, the 10th day of JULY, 1888, at Eleven o'clock in the Forenoon, and proceed to take evidence in reference to the Petition that has been presented to Her Majesty in Council, for a grant of a Charter of Incorporation to the Parish of Richmond, according to the provisions of the " Municipal Corporations' Act, 1882."

AND further, that all persons interested in the Inquiry and who may wish to give evidence before the said Commissioner, must then and there attend, and they will be heard.

Dated this 27th June, 1888.

This Notice is published by direction of the said Commissioner, by

THOS. SKEWES-COX,

Chairman of the Richmond Ratepayers' Incorporation Committee.

R. W. Simpson & Storey. Printers Marshgate, Richmond.

192. *Sir John Whittaker Ellis*, the only man to have gone on from being Lord Mayor of London to become Mayor of Richmond!.

190. The arms of the Borough of Richmond, granted in 1891, included a representation of the Tudor palace and three royal badges, the lion, the portcullis and the Tudor rose. The swan signifies the River Thames, the deer in the crest Richmond Park.

191. One of the rejected prize-winning designs for the new town hall (this won the second prize and was by T. Verity).

193. *Richmond Town Hall* in 1893.

Incorporation as a borough came in 1890. By that time Sir John Whittaker Ellis (a younger son of Joseph Ellis, and a former Lord Mayor of London) had bought up the Castle and presented it to the Vestry in 1888 as a site for a new municipal building. The design was put out to architectural competition, but the Vestry rejected both the prize-winning entries and chose instead one that, in terms of cost, had exceeded the brief. The architect was W.J. Ancell and the new Town Hall was to cost eventually twice the original competition target; it was opened by the Duke of York, the future George V, in June 1893.

The first election of the Richmond Borough Council was on 1 November 1890. Sir John Whittaker Ellis was chosen to be the first mayor. Sir Edward Hertslet, Librarian of the Foreign Office, who had been acting as 'Provisional Mayor', placed the gold chain of office (provided by Ellis himself) on the new Mayor's shoulders.

LOCAL NEWSPAPERS

Among the newly elected Councillors in 1890 was Frederick W. Dimbleby, proprietor of the *Richmond and Twickenham Times*.

Although the *Surrey Comet*, a Kingston paper founded in 1854, carried (as it still does) news of the Richmond area, a number of short-lived attempts were made in the 1850s and '60s to start papers in Richmond. The *Times* was the first to succeed and flourish. It was founded as a weekly in 1873 by Edward King, a local printer. Dimbleby, aged twenty, joined the staff in 1874; rose to become King's principal assistant; and purchased the paper when King retired in 1894. The *Richmond and Twickenham Times* is now the central member of a group of local *Times* newspapers still owned and published by the Dimbleby family.

Its main competitor, from 1885 to 1976, was the *Richmond Herald*. After 1976 this continued until 1987 as one of the free weekly papers which have proliferated in recent years.

194. *Richmond Town Hall from the river* (watercolour by C.J. Lander *c*1910).

195. Constables' truncheons and rattle (Museum of Richmond).

196. *The Richmond watch-house* in 1754, with the pound and stocks on the left.

CRIMEWATCH AND FIREWATCH

The manor courts originally policed the town, electing from among the inhabitants a constable who served, occasionally with much reluctance and negligence, but always without payment. He was supplemented, as the affairs of the town became more complex, by a paid parish beadle, for the duties now included the care and manning of the Vestry fire engines and the supervision of the night watch. A small watch-house and lock-up (similar to that still surviving in Petersham) can be seen in *The Prospect of Richmond* of 1726 (see p. 32), standing in the wide part of George Street opposite the end of Duke Street. A new watch-house and, adjacent to it, 'a convenient house...to contain the two fire engines' were built in 1730.

The maintenance of a night watch and the fighting of fires were two sides of the same coin. As was reported in 1739, 'the Watch of this Parish was only irregularly summoned...its maintenance and support were unequally levied. Many inconveniences may happen by Fire and Irregularities committed by loose and disorderly Persons in the Night during the Winter Season without any probability of being discovered till the like fatal Calamaties are past recovery.' It was agreed to have a regular watch from each November to the end of February, and to employ three fit and able night watchmen from among the 'casual poor'. In 1755 the engine house was enlarged, apparently to provide accommodation for the beadle looking after the engines.

In 1772 the Parish Trustees set up a regular watch of six men, with specified beats. The force was doubled again in 1783. The Trustees also bought a new fire engine and arranged for screws, compatible with those on the fire hoses, to be fixed to the two obelisk pumps at the ends of George Street.

The new Metropolitan Police took over responsibility for the town in 1840 and a police station was built in Princes Street; fifty years later a new building was put up in George Street, a few yards from the site of the original watch-house. When the Police Station was moved to its present location in Red Lion Street in 1912, this building was converted into shops.

197. *The Police Station* in George Street, *c*1900. One of the obelisks, with a public water pump, stood in front of it; the other was at the King Street corner.

198. *Petersham watch-house and lock-up*, beside the old building of the Fox and Duck Inn, *c*1910.

199. A manual fire engine which was supplied for use at Kew Palace in the reign of George III, with the Kew Palace fire brigade *c*1890.

200. Lead firemarks from Parkshot House, now in the Museum of Richmond (drawing by Caroline Church).

Fighting fires was still, however, the Vestry's concern. Two manual engines were kept at the watch-house, but the great problem remained their manning. Though there were volunteers – well paid when called on – the process of mustering took too long. At night they would have to be roused from their beds, at day from their employments. Moreover the water supply was inadequate, and particularly the water pressure on the Hill was too low to provide a good flow. After the disastrous fire at the Star and Garter in 1870, an attempt was made to improve things. The problems with the water company were one reason why Richmond decided to establish its own water supply (see p. 110).

But some things were capable of immediate improvement. A full-time Captain was employed for the (still basically volunteer), fire brigade. A new fire station was built in the Square which contained accommodation for stand-by firemen; this replaced the old watch-house. So far, the engines had been powered by manual pumps, but in 1875 the first steam-pump engine was bought. In 1891 a system of electric fire alarm pillars was installed throughout the town.

It was not until 1926–27 however that the fire brigade became fully professional, with eight paid firemen in addition to the Captain. In 1932 the station was moved to the old tram depot in the Kew Road and, in 1963, to the Lower Richmond Road.

201. *Richmond Fire Station* (from Somers Gascoyne's *Recollections of Richmond*, *c*1899).

202. The ruins of the Star and Garter on the morning after the fire in 1870 (from the *Illustrated London News*).

203. *The Richmond Volunteer Fire Brigade* with their two 'steamers' outside the fire station in the 1880s.

204. *Brooks's grocery store* at No 79 George Street became the Post Office in 1858.

205. *Petersham Post Office* in 1902.

GETTING THE POST

The first indication of a public postal service at Richmond is the description of Nathan Williams as 'postman' in the parish registers in 1702.

Some eighty years later Robert Rowland, a grocer of 9 King Street, was the Richmond postmaster, despatching in 1780 three mail coaches to London every day. He was succeeded by his wife and then his daughter. About 1843 the post office was moved to Mr Lloyd's, the chemist, in George Street, and fifteen years later to the grocery shop of John Brooks at 79 George Street. Brooks's widow presided over the move into the first specially built Post Office, at 70 George Street, in 1886; and her son succeeded her as postmaster. At this address, with expansions into neighbouring houses, the post office remained until it was rebuilt at the corner of Water Lane in 1980.

The frequency of collections and deliveries in the earlier days is startling. From most pillar boxes there were ten collections each weekday.

Petersham had a tiny, but independent, post office, run for many years by generations of the Long family. This was moved to the Petersham Stores in 1924, and closed in 1966.

WATER ON TAP

Apart from the conduits which took water from springs on the slopes of the Hill to the Palace and to the Charterhouse, Richmond's water supply was from wells and springs until the late seventeenth century. In 1682/3 one Peter Wally was granted a patent for the use of an engine to convey water from the Thames to the house of Sir James Butler on the lower part of Richmond Hill. When, in 1685, he applied to supply Richmond as a whole, the inhabitants were enthusiastic and he was given licence to 'lay pipes through the streets and wastes and to erect conduits and receptacles for water.'

Throughout the eighteenth century private contractors operated the waterworks by the riverside in the Petersham Road. Then, in 1835, a company was formed for the purpose. An improved pumping engine and a new water tower were installed, but the water supplied was still unfiltered and untreated river water, and by the late 1850s was becoming very polluted.

Approaches were made to some of the large companies supplying water to London, as a result of which the Southwark and Vauxhall Company (S&V) launched a take-over bid for the Richmond Water Company, despite the opposition of the local inhabitants who thought S&V's prices too high. Eventually, Richmond's water was supplied by S&V from Battersea and the Richmond waterworks were closed down.

206. Tudor collecting chamber for water conduit, Mount Ararat Road, when opened up in 1909.

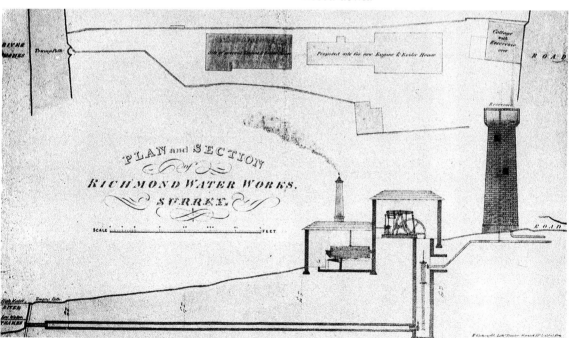

207. The new equipment for the water works in the Petersham Road, 1835 (lithograph by R. Cartwright).

RICHMOND
WATER SUPPLY.

The Southwark and Vauxhall Water Company having early on Sunday Morning, the 14th instant, cut off the Water from this Town, the Water Supply Committee of the Vestry **GIVE NOTICE** that until the several connections between the Water Mains of the Parish and the houses of the Rate-payers are completed in the several streets, **STAND PIPES** will be fixed in such streets, between 7 a.m. and 6 p.m., at short distances, for the use of the Inhabitants, and such other means as are practicable will be adopted for the convenience of the Consumers.

The Committee regret to have to state that the continued heavy rain has greatly retarded the carrying out of this part of their Works, but weather permitting, it will proceed with all possible dispatch.

All Applications respecting Water Supply should be addressed to Mr. G. STRIBLING, Inspector of Fittings and Turncock, at No. 2, Whitchurch Villas, Mount Ararat Road, Richmond.

The Committee are using their utmost endeavours to give an ample supply of Water to the Town, and confidently appeal to the Inhabitants to support them by avoiding all unnecessary use or waste of the Water.

Dated this 15th day of January, 1877.

F. B. SENIOR,
Vestry Clerk.

208. Poster warning of the water crisis in January 1877.

209. Of course, if water was not available, there was always an alternative! (The Rose and Crown on Kew Green is depicted here.)

The 1860s were filled with squabbles over the quality and price of S&V water. The Star and Garter fire underlined that there was no pressure in the mains up on the Hill. So S&V proposed a new system of increasing the pressure if alerted by electric telegraph from the Richmond fire station but the system, when tested, did not work. S&V ignored all complaints from the Vestry and when, in 1873, they doubled their prices to domestic users an indignant public meeting urged the Vestry to 'find other means to supply wholesome water at less cost.'

The Vestry, advised that S&V had no legal right to supply water to Richmond, proposed to develop its own supply based on local artesian wells. At a public enquiry into its plan in 1874 S&V's claims to monopoly were rejected; the Queen agreed to the building of a reservoir in Richmond Park; and in 1875 the Vestry's plan was given the go-ahead. The new enterprise sank new wells, but also took over the brewery in Water Lane which already had its own artesian well; it also had to lay new mains (S&V having refused to sell their own).

By December 1876 work was well advanced but several months from completion. On the 13th S&V announced that, as it appeared that they had no right to supply Richmond with water, they would discontinue their supplies on 13 January. In a race against time the Vestry pressed on feverishly with its own work, severely impeded by heavy rain which made digging difficult. As the mains were completed they were filled with water from the brewery artesian well, for the newly sunk wells were not yet yielding properly.

By 13 January the mains were almost complete, but few domestic connections had yet been made. Even so, S&V cut off the water. Standpipes were erected in the streets; the parish water carts, normally used for watering the streets, were pressed into service as drinking water bowsers; the Tudor conduit work in Mount Ararat Road was opened up; extra fire engines were borrowed to help fill the reservoir from streams in the park and from the Leg of Mutton pond (the water of which was said by the local medical officer to be of better quality than that supplied by S&V). Richmond survived the crisis, and a month later all domestic connections had been made.

Richmond continued to manage its own water supply, supplemented by a new artesian well in Terrace Gardens and by shallow wells in Petersham Meadows, until the 1960s. Latterly, however, it had become necessary to buy increasingly from the Metropolitan Water Board, to whom the whole responsibility was handed over when the Greater London Borough of Richmond upon Thames was formed in 1965.

The Open Spaces

DOWN BY THE RIVERSIDE

In the eighteenth century the walk by the river outside the site of the old Palace was a fashionable promenade. Called Cholmondeley Walk, from the mansion built there in the 1740s by the Earl of Cholmondeley, it was in fact the only stretch of the riverside where one could walk with pleasure. Upstream of the Town Wharf at the end of Water Lane, there was no riverside path at all, and private gardens stretched to the river bank. The deal which George III made for the closure of Sheen Lane in 1774 had involved him in causing 'the commodious publick foot-walk to be made along the Side of the River from the late horse-ferry at Kew to the Scite of His Majesty's ancient Palace of Richmond', but this was likely to be full of bargemen towing barges.

However, a new Act in 1777 authorised the City of London, who managed the Thames up to Staines, to build a new towpath for horses from Kew to Water Lane, which they started to extend to Richmond Bridge. This was not popular, but in July 1779, despite protest and obstructions from riverside landowners, the City authorities began the construction of a towpath from Water Lane to the Ham Walks. This was done by building the new path on the river bank, outside the boundaries of the private property, but the new piles were cut down by the protesters and George Colman of Bath House (later Northumberland House) went so far as to engage a gang of 'coalheavers, watermen, etc, armed with axes and saws' to attack the City's labourers. It took the intervention of City Marshals and a file of soldiers to suppress the trouble and arrest the delinquents. Colman retaliated by bringing a suit in the King's Bench for injury done to his premises, but lost. The path was extended, but not to Ham Walks as intended. It got only as far as the grounds of Montagu (later Buccleuch) House, for the Duke firmly refused its continuance through his gardens – and he had the influence to prevail. Though the riverside gardens of Buccleuch House were added to the public domain in 1938, there is still no direct path by the riverside through into Petersham Meadows and on to Ham.

210. *Cholmondeley Walk* as shown in an engraving from a watercolour by Augustin Heckel, 1749. The recently completed mansion of the Earl of Cholmondeley dominates the riverside walk.

211. An illuminated fête on the river at Richmond in the 1890s.

Detour around Buccleuch House or not, the new towing path soon became a delightful promenade. The railway, and then the motor buses, brought day-trippers in their thousands, and a day on and beside the river was the chief attraction. The river was exploited as an amenity and Richmond's boat-builders acquired huge fleets of rowing boats for hire. Races and regattas were common and splendid illuminated fetes were held. When the river froze hard enough, skaters even turned up to an early sort of ice-hockey.

212. The Thames frozen over in 1855 (from the *Illustrated London News*).

213. *The Richmond Amateur Regatta* in 1846. Coxed fours racing past Buccleuch House (lithograph from a drawing by W. Pascoe).

214. *The Richmond Regatta* in the 1890s

215. Boats for hire at Richmond, early this century.

216. An election print depicting Sir Robert Walpole as the 'English Colossus', 1740.

RICHMOND PARK

In 1727 Robert, Lord Walpole, eldest son of the prime minister, Sir Robert Walpole, became Ranger of Richmond Park, and his father hunted there once or twice a week. Sir Robert took over Hartleton Lodge in the southern part of the Park and spent his own money in turning it into a country mansion, thenceforward known simply as 'Old Lodge'.

At this very time a 'New Lodge' was being built, begun in the last year of George I's life, to the Palladian design of Roger Morris, protégé of Lord Herbert, later Earl of Pembroke. Work on the new house, sited a little to the north of Hartleton Lodge, was completed by George II. It was a small building, really intended as a place for a meal and a rest during the hunt, rather than a place to stay. Faced with Portland stone, it became known as the White Lodge. Queen Caroline liked it and in 1736–37 the 'Queen's private road' was constructed across the Richmond fields and Sheen Common to link it directly to Richmond Lodge.

Walpole also enlarged a former gamekeeper's lodge and built a thatched summer house in its grounds from which it acquired the name of Thatched House Lodge. New gatekeepers' lodges and a summer-house pavilion on the brow of the hill overlooking the river were erected. In all, he spent some £14,000 on improvements to the Park, which he used regularly as a weekend retreat.

217. *Old Lodge* in Richmond Park (engraving by W. Watts from a painting by George Barrett R.A., 1780).

218. *White Lodge,* with the pavilions added in 1754 (drawn by J. Gandon and engraved by T. Miller for Volume IV of *Vitruvius Britannicus*).

219. The thatched summer house at Thatched House Lodge.

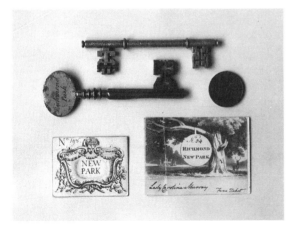

220. Keys and tickets for Richmond Park (Museum of Richmond).

The royal family often joined in the stag hunts, or in shooting wild turkeys of which a flock was raised in the Park as game birds. So many people came to watch (access to the Park for the local population had been virtually unlimited since its enclosure) that in 1735 they were considered 'not only troublesome but very dangerous', and a notice was issued that entrance in future would only be allowed to those with a 'hunting ticket', to be obtained from the Ranger.

Then came further restrictions. Tickets were required for carriages; the locks on the gates were changed so that those who were previously keyholders now had to go to the lodges and show their tickets to enter the park. In what was known as 'Fence Month', allegedly to protect the young deer, almost nobody, ticket holder or not, was admitted.

George II's daughter, Princess Amelia, became Ranger after Lord Walpole and imposed further restrictions. But on 16 May 1751 there was an incident. The parish party performing the annual ritual of beating the bounds of Richmond found that the ladders usually placed to enable them to cross the wall and so continue along the parish boundary within the park were not there. (There had once been a pedestrian gate but that had been closed some years before.) Whether the party broke down the wall or found a place where it was already broken is not quite clear, but the upshot was that the Princess in future denied access to all but her guests. The issue of carriage tickets was very restricted (even the Lord Chancellor was refused) and pedestrians were kept out altogether.

Petitions to the Princess and letters to the press failed to change things. Some local gentlemen tried the issue by bringing a gatekeeper to court. The suit, which claimed a right of way 'for horses, coaches, carts, carriages and people on foot', was decided in favour of the defendant, but there was a strong hint that a case limited to a right of footway might have succeeded. John Lewis, a Richmond

221. John Lewis, the Richmond brewer, who won the battle for pedestrian access to the Park (engraving from a portrait in the Old Town Hall).

brewer, who was probably the author of a series of anonymous pamphlets protesting at the restrictions, now brought a case himself to establish the right of pedestrian access. At Kingston Assizes in 1758 he was successful, and ladder-stiles were set up again. Lewis became a local hero – and the Princess gave up the Rangership in 1761.

Sir John Soane was responsible for a number of additions to the Park. He designed the new gates and lodge built in the 1790s at the Richmond Gate, he enlarged the former 'molekeeper's house' or Hill Lodge, for Elizabeth, Countess of Pembroke, and he also improved Thatched House Lodge. These two converted lodges became houses for gentry and nobility, as did also the former 'Dog Kennels' by the Sheen Gate, which became Sheen Pond Lodge, and was occupied for sixty-five years by the Adam family and then for sixty-nine years by the family of Sir Richard Owen, first Director of the Natural History Museum.

White Lodge was granted by George III to Henry Addington (later Viscount Sidmouth) who, in 1801, had just succeeded Pitt as prime minister. The house was enlarged again for him and remained his country seat until his death in 1844. He also held the post of Deputy Ranger of the Park and it was he

222. The bounds-beating party effects an entry into Richmond Park in May 1751 (frontispiece to *Two Historical Accounts of…New Forest…and Richmond New Park*).

who supervised an extensive new policy of plantations. Another prime minister was later to live in the Park, for in 1847 Pembroke Lodge was granted to Lord John (later Earl) Russell. It remained a home of the Russell family until 1901. Lord John's grandson, Bertrand Russell, spent much of his childhood there.

Old Lodge, in bad condition, was demolished by 1841. White Lodge was granted in 1869 to Princess Mary of Cambridge and her new husband the Duke of Teck – the parents of the future Queen Mary. Edward VIII was born there in 1894.

From the 1850s restrictions on carriage entry and on the areas where pedestrians might walk were progressively abandoned, and by 1872 it was accepted that the public should enjoy the royal parks, a view shared by Edward VII who instructed his managers to make this more possible.

Richmond Park is a story of 'ifs'. If Charles I had not enclosed the Park it might by now have been built over. If Parliament had not given it to the City of London it might not have gone back intact to the Crown. If John Lewis had not won his suit for pedestrian access it might have become wholly private royal property. Richmond should be thankful.

224. *Pembroke Lodge* when occupied by Lord John Russell (from the *Illustrated News of the World*, 1858).

223. The new terrace formed at the crest of the hill after the land in 'Petersham Park' had been restored to Richmond Park in 1835 (engraved by Frederick Smith for Cooke's *The Beauties of Richmond and its Surrounding Scenery*).

225. *Sir William Hooker*, a portrait by S. Gambardella, *c*1843.

KEW GARDENS

George IV, who had a short-lived scheme for replacing the Castellated Palace and the Dutch House with a new building, added Hunter House (now the herbarium) to the royal estate in 1820, and then enclosed the western end of Kew Green in 1823. Some of the enclosed land was returned to the Green by William IV.

It was shortly after Victoria came to the throne that a Parliamentary Commission recommended that the gardens at Kew should become a national botanic garden, and the Queen agreed. On 1 April 1841 Sir William Hooker, Professor of Botany at Glasgow, became the first Director of the Royal Botanic Gardens under the aegis of the Commissioners of Woods and Forests, and his first action was to open the gardens freely to the public every weekday afternoon.

Initially Hooker's domain was only the nine acres of Princess Augusta's botanic garden, but he was soon given extra ground. A few acres between the original garden and the grounds of Kew Palace, added in 1842, made possible the erection of the new entrance gates on Kew Green. In the following year 46 acres were added on the south side, which allowed Hooker to plan a great Palm House, designed by Decimus Burton, with contributions from Richard Turner, the ironmaster who built the wrought-iron frame. In 1845 the whole of the former

226. *The Palm House at Kew* in the 1850s (drawn by W. Lacey and engraved by H. Adlard).

Richmond Gardens and Kew Gardens, except the Palace and the Queen's Cottage (and the King of Hanover's game preserve, not surrendered until 1849) were made over to Hooker. He got William Nesfield, a garden-architect, to plan a new layout with long walks and vistas.

A museum was opened in 1847; and when the King of Hanover (George III's son) died his house, the former Hunter House, became the library and herbarium. Ten years later the Temperate House, also designed by Burton, was opened, and when a great deal of gravel was needed to consolidate the terrace on which the Temperate House stands, Hooker had the idea of turning the gravel pits into a new lake.

Hooker's son, Sir Joseph, who succeeded him, emphasised the research function of the Gardens. He tried in vain to oppose the public demand for admission before 1pm each day, deploring 'the tendency to regard the Gardens as a resort for pleasure seekers', but in 1882 he had to give way and agree to open at noon. By 1921 the Gardens were opened from 10am all year round to the public. A penny admission charge was levied in 1916, increased to 3d in 1951 and reduced to one new penny in 1971: admission is now £3!

The 1980s have seen the most extensive work on buildings in the Gardens since their opening, with the complete restoration of the Palm House, and the completion of the Princess of Wales Conservatory in 1987 and the Sir Joseph Banks Building in 1990.

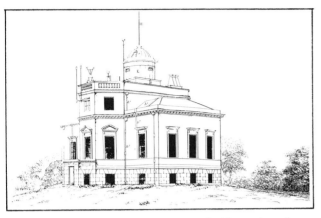

227. *The King's Observatory* equipped with a variety of meteorological instruments in 1844 (from the *Report of the Fourteenth Meeting of the British Association for the Advancement of Science*).

228. International rugby match between England and Scotland at the Athletics Ground, Richmond, in 1891.

THE OLD DEER PARK

When Richmond and Kew Gardens were taken over by the Commissioners of Woods in 1840, the whole southern end of the royal estate, which had included the deer park, was still open farm land. The Observatory was threatened with demolition and the royal scientific collections kept in it were dispersed. The Observatory was however saved by the British Association for the Advancement of Science, for use as a laboratory for electrical and meteorological experiments. From 1851 it standardised and checked the accuracy of scientific instruments, and in 1867 became the central observation station for the new Meteorological Office. The National Physical Laboratory was founded there in 1900, but moved to Bushy Park in 1910. The Meteorological Office remained until 1980, when the building was converted to office use.

The Old Deer Park land was leased to a tenant farmer, but in 1862 the newly-formed Richmond Cricket Club took ten acres by the Kew Road. Then in 1885 another nine acres were leased for the 'Athletics ground'. Several times enlarged, this became a venue for international rugby and hockey and for the Richmond Royal Horse Show, held annually from 1892 to 1967. Both grounds were used for many other sports as well.

The Richmond Golf Club played on a 9-hole course rented from the farmer for a couple of months in 1891, then moved on to Sudbrook; but in the following year the Mid-Surrey Golf Club leased all the farm land for a new course; Richmond Council took the eighty-seven acres left over for a recreation ground in 1898.

229. *The Royal Richmond Horse Show*

230. Poster for one of the first motor shows ever held in Britain (in 1899).

RICHMOND HILL AND THE TERRACE GARDENS

The land which had once been Richmond Wells, with the addition of the 'Tile Kiln Ground' and other parts of the Hill Common, had become, by the early nineteenth century, the grounds of three mansions: Cardigan House, on the site of some of the Wells buildings; Lansdowne House, opposite the end of Friars Stile Road; and Buccleuch House by the riverside. What was left of Hill Common, with the Terrace at its upper side, and Petersham Common had become favourite places for walks, for admiring the river, and for picnics.

In 1870 the Duke of Buccleuch bought the riverside land attached to Lansdowne House (the house itself was demolished by 1875, when the Duke also purchased most of its grounds on the hillside). When Buccleuch's son put the estate up for sale in 1884 the Vestry was keen to buy but couldn't afford the price. So Sir John Whittaker Ellis made a deal with them. He would buy the house for himself, retaining only the land between the river and the Petersham Road and the Vestry would purchase all the land on the hillside. In 1887 the land bought by the Vestry was opened by the Duchess of Teck as the new Terrace Gardens.

Richmond Council bought the Buccleuch House itself in 1937 and demolished it, leaving the riverside gardens open to the public. The grotto tunnel, built beneath the Petersham Road by the Duke of Montagu in the eighteenth century to connect two parts of his grounds, could once more be used for this purpose. Though Cardigan House survived until 1970 as a clubhouse for the British Legion, its gardens were added to the Terrace Gardens in the 1950s.

With the opening of Terrace Gardens, the remaining part of Hill Common (now called Terrace Field), which had been leased out as pasture, was also opened up to the public. Nightingale Lane, which bounds it on two sides and which was constructed in 1810, reminds us that Richmond Hill was once renowned for the song of its nightingales. Wordsworth wrote a sonnet about them in 1820. But, alas, his 'choir of Richmond Hill, chanting with indefatigable bill,' is no more.

231. *'Pic-Nic-Ing on Richmond Hill'* was the title of this etching by P. Egan jnr in 1838.

232. The opening of the Terrace Gardens, 1887

233. *Cardigan House* (from a sale catalogue, 1867).

234. *Lansdowne House* (from a sale catalogue 1868).

Writers in Richmond

CHARLES DICKENS was a regular summer visitor to Petersham for some years from 1839. Then he rented Woodbine Cottage, but from 1840 onwards regularly used Elm Cottage (later enlarged to Elm Lodge). He was also well-known at the Star and Garter Hotel where he gave an annual dinner for friends on his wedding anniversary.

GEORGE ELIOT (Mary Ann Evans) lived from 1855 to 1859 with the celebrated critic George Henry Lewes at No. 8 Parkshot, an early eighteenth century terrace house which was demolished in 1900. Here she first assumed the pen-name of George Eliot, and here she began to write novels, including *Amos Barton*, *Scenes from Clerical Life*, and *Adam Bede* (finished after moving to Wandsworth).

236. *Charles Dickens*, aged 27, in the year he first came to Petersham (from a painting by D. Maclise).

235. *George Eliot*, chalk drawing by Sir Frederick W. Burton.

237. *No. 8 Parkshot*, the home of George Eliot.

MARY ELIZABETH BRADDON, a prolific novelist, had lived with John Maxwell, her first publisher, at Lichfield House in Sheen Road, for some years before she married him in 1874. Her most famous book was *Lady Audley's Secret*; another best-seller was *John Marchmont's Legacy*. These both provided names for roads off King's Road, Richmond, developed by Maxwell. Mary Braddon lived at Lichfield House until her death in 1915.

VIRGINIA WOOLF and her husband Leonard lived in Richmond from 1914 to 1924. For a few months they rented rooms at 17 The Green, then took a lease of Hogarth House (at that time only half of the mid-eighteenth-century house now known by that name, which they purchased in 1920). The Hogarth Press, which they started in the house, published some forty books in Richmond, including not only Virginia's own writings, but works by T.S. Eliot, John Middleton Murry, Sigmund Freud, and translations of Russian books.

238. *Mary Elizabeth Braddon.*

240. *Virginia Woolf.*

239. *Hogarth House, Paradise Road.* When the Woolfs lived there it was divided into two houses, Hogarth House being on the right. From 1920 they owned the entire building.

1900 – 1945

NEW THEATRES AND CINEMAS

The Georgian theatre on the Green was demolished in 1884–5 and for five years there was a hiatus. Then, in 1889, F.C. Mouflet, proprietor of the Greyhound Hotel, who also owned the Assembly Rooms of the old Castle Hotel, converted the banqueting room of the Castle into the New Theatre, as it was first called. This opened on Easter Monday 1890; patronised by royal residents it quickly changed its name, in 1891, to the Theatre Royal.

Mouflet soon found that the resources and facilities at the converted building were very restricted, and decided to replace it by a new purpose-built theatre. He acquired a site on Little Green, between the Public Library and the College, and commissioned the leading theatre architect, Frank Matcham, to design the new building with seating for about 1500 people. It was opened on 18 September 1899 as the Richmond Theatre and Opera House. It has flourished for ninety years and most celebrated actors and actresses have played on its boards – especially when it was used frequently for pre-West End runs. At the time of writing it is closed for restoration and enlargement.

The Castle Assembly Rooms reverted to their original purpose until 1910 when they were sold and reopened as Richmond's first cinema – the Castle Electric Theatre. There was seating for 500, and admission prices were threepence, sixpence and one shilling, with free teas served for the latter prices. The name Electric was dropped in 1916, but the cinema remained as the Castle Theatre until 1921.

241. *'The New Theatre at Richmond, 1890'* in the Castle Assembly Rooms (from the *Illustrated Sporting and Dramatic News*).

The Theatre,
Richmond on-Thames

242. Playbill for the opening performance at the new theatre on 18 September 1899.

243. The new Richmond Theatre on Little Green. (The cannon was a Russian one captured in the Crimean War.)

1911 saw the opening of three new cinemas: The Palace in Dome Buildings, which later became the Empire and lasted until 1922; the Pictorial Hall (1911–21) just round the corner in the Sheen Road, in the building which later became the Richmond Community Centre and then a synagogue; and the first purpose-built cinema, the Talbot Picture Theatre, which opened in April 1911 on part of the site occupied by the Talbot Hotel.

244. *The Talbot Picture Theatre*, Richmond's first purpose-built cinema, flourished from 1911 to 1930.

245. The auditorium of the Richmond Kinema (now the Odeon) when it was first opened in 1930.

246. *The Gaumont Cinema*, formerly the Royalty, at No. 5 Hill Street.

On Christmas Eve 1914 the New Royalty Kinema was opened at 5 Hill Street. An auditorium had been built in the back garden of this early eighteenth century house which was itself used as a foyer (with an open fire in winter) and tea room. The Royalty was the only one of the early cinemas to survive beyond World War II. In 1944 it was bought by the Rank Organisation and, as the Gaumont, stayed open until 1980.

Two new super-cinemas were opened in the 1930s. Joseph Mears, who owned both the Talbot and the Royalty, opened the Richmond Kinema, between the Talbot and Ormond Road, in April 1930; the subsequent demolition of the Talbot allowed the widening of Hill Street. The Richmond Kinema had to be renamed as the Premier in World War II (when all names indicative of place were banned lest they should help enemy invaders). When Mears sold out to Rank in 1944 it again had a new name, the Odeon. It still survives, though now divided into three auditoriums.

The Ritz (ABC from 1963) was opened in the Sheen Road, on a site which had been part of the grounds of Carrington Lodge, in May 1939. It was closed in 1971 and later replaced by the office building called Spencer House.

247. The first aircraft made in Richmond by the Whitehead Aircraft Co. Ltd in November 1915 was a BE2b twin-seater biplane.

248. *The London Scottish Regiment* marching into camp in Richmond Park, in May 1915.

THE WAR OF 1914–18

Though a large military camp and a Royal Flying Corps depot were established in Richmond Park, and some of the park land there and in the Old Deer Park was converted for allotments and other agricultural purposes, the main impact of the 1st World War in Richmond was that made by the wounded. Apart from the Star and Garter Home, there were military wards in the Royal Hospital and the Workhouse Infirmary; Old Friars and Old Palace Place on the Green were converted into a military hospital; and a South African War Hospital was built in Richmond Park (finally demolished in 1925). In 1918 work began on an American Red Cross Hospital in the Park, but this was discontinued at the Armistice.

A Richmond contribution to the war was military aircraft. Even before the war Richmond had had an aircraft factory in an old drill hall taken over in April 1912 by the aircraft designer R.L. Howard-Flanders, but his company lasted only a year or so. The same

premises, in Townshend Terrace, just south of the railway, were acquired in 1915 by the Whitehead Aircraft Company. Here, during the war, mostly Sopwith 'Pup' scouts and DH9 bombers were made; the works expanded with new buildings in Grena Road and Manor Park. In 1922, however, the company collapsed and the works were sold.

A lasting reminder of the War was the establishment in the Petersham Road of the British Legion poppy factory. This was in the former Watney's brewery, but was rebuilt in 1970. The Armistice Day poppies are still made there.

249. *The Church of St Philip and All Saints* in North Sheen was built in 1929 by the re-erection of a sixteenth-century barn moved from a farm in Surrey.

DEVELOPMENT BETWEEN THE WARS

The inter-war period saw new housing estates developed in North Sheen, east of the railway, from Sheen Road northwards, and the last remaining open land along and near the Kew Road was filled with new houses, with more along the road between Petersham and Ham. The Ham Urban District was included in the Borough of Richmond in 1933.

In the 1930s several very large blocks of flats were built. Queensberry House by the river gave way to flats in 1934; the site of Lichfield House in the Sheen Road was taken by Lichfield Court in the following year; Stawell House at the corner of Queen's Road and Sheen Road was demolished for the great Courtlands development; and large nineteenth-century villas on the Hill were replaced by Richmond Hill Court.

A major change in Richmond's geography was wrought in the 1930s. This was the construction of 'the Great Chertsey Road', a new main route to London so-called though it was never completed as far as Chertsey. It required two new bridges over the Thames (Chiswick Bridge and Twickenham Bridge at Richmond), the widening of the Lower Mortlake Road with the demolition of a lot of old houses and small cottages, and the construction of a highway through the southern end of the Old Deer Park.

250. Pensford Avenue, North Sheen.

The New TWICKENHAM BRIDGE at Richmond 1933.

251. *The new Twickenham Bridge at Richmond* opened in 1933 as part of the Great Chertsey Road project (etching by R. Myerscough-Walker).

252. *Lower Mortlake Road* after its widening. The Richmond gas works can be seen in the distance.

253. The new railway station at Richmond opened in 1937.

Twickenham Bridge, designed by Alfred Dryland (engineer) and Maxwell Ayrton (architect) was constructed in ferro-concrete with three wide river spans and two roadway arches, one on each bank. It was opened by the Prince of Wales on 3 July 1933. Its completion eventually allowed the long-needed widening of Richmond Bridge.

Soon after, in 1936–37, Richmond Station was rebuilt to serve both the District and North London terminals and the through tracks of what was now the Southern Railway.

254. An emergency water supply tank at the corner of Richmond Green.

THE SECOND WORLD WAR

This war had a greater impact on Richmond than that of 1914–18. Richmond Green was torn up for an air raid shelter and Kew Green for a wardens' post. Large water tanks were installed and pipelines built from the river to Richmond Green and up the slopes of Terrace Field to the top of the Hill.

Richmond suffered quite severely from bombing. Incendiary bombs burnt out the Town Hall and the adjacent bank in November 1940. Landmarks such as the Wesleyan Chapel in Friars Stile Road, Sheen Pond Lodge in Richmond Park and the Russell School in Petersham were all destroyed in other raids, and the new Courtlands flats suffered a devastating direct hit. In all, 297 houses were destroyed and nearly twelve thousand damaged. Ninety-seven people were killed in Richmond and some 500 injured.

Over in Richmond Park most of the pastures and playing fields were ploughed up for crops. The Pen Ponds were drained and camouflaged. There were anti-aircraft emplacements in the Park, and a military camp occupied about fifty acres near the southwest corner. This camp, not finally demolished until the 1960s, was used for the Olympic Village when the Games came to London in 1948.

255. Preparation for war: construction of an air-raid shelter in Richmond Green in September 1938.

256. Bombing: the Courtlands flats in Sheen Road.

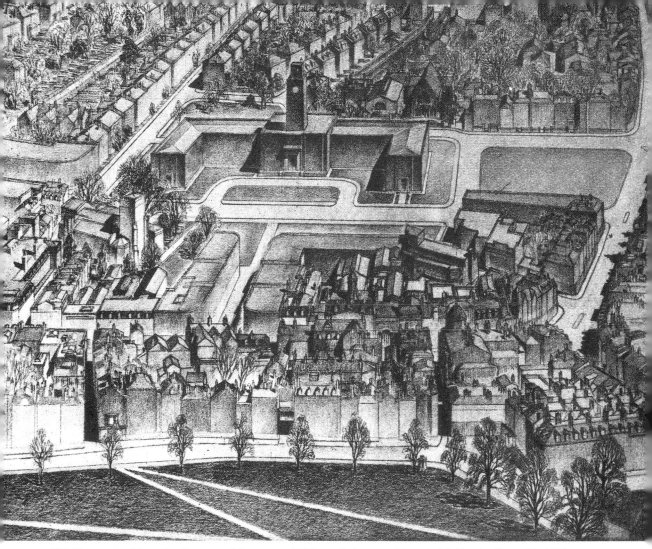

257. The proposal for redevelopment of the centre of Richmond, 'approved in principle' by the Council in 1945.

Modern Times

Richmond was not immune from the fever of vision-ary replanning that beset London and other cities as the war drew to a close. But it was fortunate to escape implementation of the new town centre pro-ject presented in 1945 which involved the building of a new civic centre opposite the end of the bridge, to which almost everything in the area, including some of Richmond's best old houses, would have been sacrificed.

Another scheme, which persisted until the 1970s, was for a new highway from Queen's Road, passing in a tunnel under the corner of the Park near Rich-mond Gate, clipping off a corner of the Richmond Golf Club's course at Sudbrook, by-passing Peter-sham altogether, and joining up with the Kingston Road near Ham Common.

The physical changes that have taken place have mostly been a continuation of the inter-war trends – the demolition of large mansions (Northumberland House and Cardigan House for example) and the conversion or replacement of the larger nineteenth-century villas. New shops and new schools have appeared. But the principal difference has been the construction of many large office buildings and an influx of office workers – there are now commuters *to* Richmond.

But Richmond has largely avoided high-rise buildings and within the old Richmond area there are, in fact, only three. Two of these are at Peldon Court, a Council housing project of the late 1950s in an area off the Sheen Road where some fifty houses had been badly damaged or destroyed in the war, and the third is The Towers in the Lower Mortlake Road – a reconstructed part of 'New Richmond'.

Richmond itself was merged into a much larger borough in 1965 – Richmond upon Thames now

258. New office buildings in Paradise Road: Eton House in the foreground.

260. *Peldon Court* flats.

includes also the former boroughs of Twickenham and of Barnes and Mortlake, and is the only London Borough to span both sides of the Thames. The municipal headquarters were located in Twickenham; but Richmond residents could rejoice in the new name.

259. *Dickens and Jones* store in George Street, which replaced Gosling's in 1970.

261. *St Richard's at Ham*, with the new St Richard's school on the right.

DEVELOPMENTS AT HAM

While Petersham has escaped large-scale redevelopment Ham has altered greatly in character. The old part along Ham Street and around the Common retains much of its charm, but to the west, all is changed. A considerable part of the old fields had been exploited by the Dysarts of Ham House as gravel pits in the first half of this century. Most of this area, though leaving a fringe of riverside meadows, was covered with flats and houses in the 1960s in a Wates development, in the centre of which is a striking new church, St Richard's, consecrated in 1967.

262. Part of the Wates estate at Ham.

The Bishop of Kingston, to whom fell the task of deciding on the dedication of the church, explained that he had tried to find a Surrey saint, but apparently there wasn't one. So he had settled for a Sussex one: Richard de Wiche, a thirteenth-century Bishop of Chichester.

Another large development scheme in Ham was the Parkleys Estate, built by Span in 1953–56 to the designs of Eric Lyons. This lies to the south of Ham Common on the eastern side of Upper Ham Road.

263. Flats at Ham Close.

264. Houses in Reynolds Place, Queen's Road Estate, built by the London and Quadrant Housing Association, and completed in 1983.

THE QUEEN'S ROAD ESTATE

The leases granted by the Vestry for the 'Parish Lands' in Queen's Road all fell in between 1940 and 1962. There was considerable interest in how the estate would be redeveloped and in the application of the increased income expected – in the past the income had gone to support the poor rate and, in effect, subsidised the ratepayers, but only those in the parish of Richmond. There was much concern that the Council (who were now the Trustees of the charity) would let it to the developers with the highest bid; and a pressure group led by the Vicar tried to persuade them to develop it to meet community housing needs. When the Vicar, Canon Landreth, was told by a leading Conservative member of the Council that he should not interfere in the business of *elected* representatives, he stood for the Council himself as an independent. He – and other supporters of the cause – were elected; and the Conservatives lost their overall control of the Council. The battle was half-won; but two court cases in 1965 resulted in the eventual reconstitution of the old Charity with far wider charitable purposes, and the appointment of new Trustees.

The new Trustees proposed a mixed development, containing houses, a few small flats and sheltered accommodation, all to be leased at fair rents. With the help of the government's Housing Cor-

265. *Fitzherbert House*: sheltered accommodation replacing one of the old workhouse infirmary blocks on the Queen's Road Estate.

poration and of the London and Quadrant Housing Association, they have been able to carry through most (but not yet all) of it. The old workhouse was sold, the smaller properties in Cambrian and Chisholm Roads retained and restored. As a result of leases and sales the Charity now disposes of a large sum of capital, from the income on which it has been able both to assist major community projects and to make innumerable small grants to deserving charitable bodies and individuals.

266. The Richmond riverside in 1959.

BACK TO THE RIVERSIDE

From 1960, when Hotham House by the river collapsed, and when there were plans to redevelop the
Palm Court Hotel next door, the block of property
between Bridge Street and Water Lane suffered
from planning blight for twenty-five years. A succession of developers and local bodies produced a
variety of schemes – all of them rejected by the planning authorities – ranging from a seventeen-storey
block of flats to a community centre with concert
halls, restaurants and a hotel. There were conflict-
ing interests; the conservationists on the one hand
wanted the retention of Heron House and Tower
House, the Town Hall (which ceased to be used as
such in 1965) and the Castle Assembly Rooms, but
the developers wanted intensive development. For
others the priority was an overall gain in amenity
and a visually attractive scheme.

In the early 1980s two smaller schemes of renovation were successfully carried out: the restoration
and conversion of Riverside House (the old Waterworks office), and the renovation of 5 Hill Street and
the building of Centenary House on the site of the
Gaumont Cinema auditorium – a scheme, inciden-
tally, which has produced Richmond's only new
cinema since the 1930s, the small Richmond Film-
house in Water Lane, opened in 1990. The future of
the main site, however, remained in doubt until

Haslemere Estates obtained the Council's approval
for their plan in 1984.

This was for a complex of buildings, all designed
by Quinlan Terry, in a variety of classical and Georgian styles, to incorporate some at least of the old
buildings. Heron House was to be preserved as a
reminder of the 1690s; Tower House, built in 1856,
with the campanile so long part of the view of the
bridge, would be retained, as would the 1820s
facade of the houses that had once been the Royal
Hotel. The Town Hall was to be renovated, enlarged and used (except for a shop on the ground
floor front) for community purposes. The whole of
Royal Terrace however was to be demolished, as
were the Castle Assembly Rooms (to be replaced by
an office building whose design owed a lot to one of
Chambers' palace projects (p. 31). Most of the new
buildings would be offices with shops at street level
on the Hill and Bridge Street frontages, but some
new flats were to be built on Water Lane.

The new development was opened by the Queen
on 28 October 1988.

In the restored Town Hall, which was to house
the Central Reference Library, the Council allotted
space for a museum of local history. A group of
Richmond residents pursued the project, formed a
Company, raised the funds necessary by public

appeal and from grants and sponsorships, and was able to set up the Museum of Richmond in time for the Queen to open it formally on the same day. Those who want to see more of the history of Richmond, illustrated with objects as well as pictures, should pay it a visit.

The museum project is but one of many new initiatives which demonstrate both a continuing awareness of a Richmond identity within the new larger borough and the willingness of many inhabitants to play an active part in the preservation and development of the town's amenities. Several of Richmond's traditions combine in these activities: its long cultural heritage, its lively sense of community care, its record of vigorous and successful popular protests (of which the water supply issue and the Parish Lands dispute mentioned earlier are two examples among many).

New groups and societies have proliferated in the last twenty or thirty years, in charitable, cultural and artistic fields – and to protect and support amenities. Music and drama flourish – the fringe theatre at the Orange Tree pub has been so successful that it has now moved into a newly-built theatre. Groups of 'Friends' not only support Richmond Theatre, the Orange Tree, the Museum, Richmond Park, etc., but spring up fully armed to counter any threat to familiar and cherished buildings or institutions,

267. The opening of the Museum of Richmond by Her Majesty the Queen on 28 October 1988. With the Queen is the author, Chairman of the Museum. Kate Thaxton, the Museum's first Curator, is behind; and Robin Wade, the designer of the Museum, is just visible on the right.

whether from developers, authorities, neglect or fair wear and tear. Just to see all these groups' stands at events such as the annual May Fair on Richmond Green or the Kew Fair is proof that Richmond is far from being a dormitory suburb. It remains a community, proud of its history and of its character, and determined to protect and enhance them.

268. Inside the Museum of Richmond. The clock mechanism, made in 1819, was formerly used at the old workhouse. The clock face is still on the building but the works were renewed in 1975. At far left is the corner of a large model of Richmond Palace as it was in Queen Elizabeth's reign.

269. The new riverside development at Richmond designed by Quinlan Terry, and built by Haslemere Estates.

INDEX

Page numbers in bold type
indicate illustrations.